POWER IN ICA

The Structural History
of a Peruvian Community

A Latin American Case Study

Under the editorship of MAY N. DIAZ

POWER IN ICA

The Structural History
of a Peruvian Community

E. A. HAMMEL   *University of California, Berkeley*

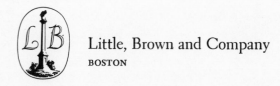

Little, Brown and Company
BOSTON

For Ken and Bruce
who remember the sand hill

Foreword

With this book we inaugurate our Latin American series, a set of anthropological case studies. The series is designed to bring to the student a number of works, each with its own focus, and all of which fit together to provide some degree of geographical coverage and the consideration of a range of scientific problems. Each book examines a particular institution or segment of a culture against the wider background of the social life and cultural processes of a community or region. It is hoped not only that the series can be useful to readers interested in learning more about the anthropology of Latin America, but also that each work will contribute to the comparative studies of social and cultural institutions.

Anthropological studies of Latin American communities have contributed many ideas and concepts that have become useful generally in social anthropology. The dramatic example of culture contact between Spaniard and Indian and the interesting evidences of syncretism among Iberian, Indian, and Afro-American cultures aroused the interest of scholars, and from the 1930's on studies in Latin America sharpened the understanding of acculturation processes.

It was in part as a result of fieldwork in Mexico that Robert Redfield postulated the "folk-urban continuum," and in the debate that followed there gradually emerged the concept of a "peasant society," a societal type characterized neither by the usual institutions of tribal societies nor by those of complex industrial ones. Among the pioneers of anthropological peasant studies, George M. Foster, who had also worked in Mexico, made clear the interrelationship and interdependence of the urban and peasant sectors in such societies.

Economic anthropology owes much to those who have worked in Latin America, and particularly in Guatemala, southern Mexico, and the Caribbean. Studies of markets and exchange provided the data and the analyses that made possible more sophisticated models of marketing systems in nonindustrial societies. This work also contributed to the understanding of the ways in which economic and social institutions affect each other.

In studying Latin American communities, anthropologists have developed models of social integration that have been useful for other societies not based primarily on kinship. Thus, out of studies of fictive kinship and *compadrazgo*, of patron-client relations, of informal social contracts, of the civil-religious hierarchy have developed models of social integration with an applicability wider than Latin America.

Recent research explores such areas as social stratification, economic development, family structure, and conflict resolution. This book is one such work; it is concerned with the stratification system of the Ica Valley of Peru, examining the interrelationship of wealth, power, and prestige. It is a study with time-depth, moving from pre-Columbian times through the colonial period and to the present, tracing the shifts that have taken place as the source of political power changed, as the agricultural system adapted to variations in the market and demands for goods, and as the definition of prestige and the cultural traits which symbolized it were altered.

Eugene A. Hammel is Professor of Anthropology at the University of California, Berkeley. His work in the areas of kinship, formal analysis, and social stratification has been published extensively. His most recent writing has been concerned with occupational mobility in Yugoslavia.

MAY N. DIAZ

Preface

This book was originally written as my doctoral dissertation in anthropology and published a few years later in condensed form.[1] In the ten years that have elapsed since the original fieldwork, I have had the opportunity to analyze and write up data not included in the first book, to compare that field trip with subsequent ones in Mexico, the Southwestern United States, and the Balkans, and to take advantage of the criticisms of my colleagues. Most of all, I have had the opportunity to reflect on just what it was that I did in Peru and how I might do things differently if I were to return. A great deal has happened to the Ica Valley since I left it, as well as to its ethnographer; I have tried in this revision to bring the information up to date through further research in Peruvian published sources and through consultation with others who know the

[1] Hammel 1959, 1962a. The University of New Mexico Press has kindly consented to this revision. In this work I have tried to strike a compromise between the needs of the social science instructor for supplementary readings on a particular area, of the student for a sociohistorical account that would not baffle him with technicalities and yet would indicate that social process was complex, and of the specialist whose desire it would be to examine the argument critically and minutely and to use the basic data and references to further his own research. To these ends, I have kept technical jargon to a minimum, realizing that the specialist will comprehend the specific theoretical implications of many empirical generalizations, and I have put statistical obstacles and other impedimenta into the notes, so that the specialist can find them and the general student can read around them.

valley. I am greatly indebted to Andrei Simic for his help in examining the Latin American literature for points which would help to place the work in a more comparative framework.

The original fieldwork was carried out from July 1957 to June 1958. Most of the ethnographic data came from interviews with informants and from my daily participation in the life of the valley, but I also made extensive use of local archival materials. Through the generosity of Dr. Gabriel Escobar, who with Dr. Edward Wellin had conducted studies of the public health program in Ica in 1951–1953, I was able to use some of the field notes of that project, and I also had access to the field notes and diary of Abel Muchaypiña García, field assistant to Escobar and Wellin, later a rural public health visitor in the valley, and still later my principal informant, guide, and friend. Dr. John Rowe has been generous of his time, from the inception of the project to our most recent conversations on what has happened to Ica during the last decade, and he was most helpful in providing the notes and results of his own historical and archaeological research in the area.

The field research was supported by a Research Training Fellowship from the Social Science Research Council and by an additional grant from the Research Committee of the University of California, Berkeley. The writing of the original work and of later analyses, including this one, was aided by grants from the Social Science Research Council, the Research Committees at Berkeley and at the University of New Mexico, and by a fellowship at the Center for Advanced Study in the Behavioral Sciences in Palo Alto.

People are more important to an anthropologist than funds; I am grateful to the directors and staffs of the above organizations for their patience and flexibility. I am also indebted to Harry Basehart, Gerald Berthoud, Lloyd Fallers, George Foster, Ynez Haase, William Mangin, James Parsons, David Schneider, Leslie Spier, and many others for their comments along the way. In Peru, I owed much to the courtesy and willing cooperation of the Área de Salud de Ica, to the staff of the United States Operations Mission in Lima, and to Dr. and Sra. Escobar. My work in Ica was aided immeasurably by the friendship and intelligent cooperation of Abel Muchaypiña G. and Jorge Moquillaza P. For their assistance and gracious hospitality, I am also indebted to the staff of the Anderson, Clayton Company in Ica, Isaac Barnechea M., Ismael Benavides Q., Lyndon Evelyn, R. A. Rawlins and his family, and Pablo Soldi. I owe particular thanks to Duncan Masson and his mother, Mrs. Jean Masson, whose hospitality and generous friendship have often provided Californians with a safe harbor in Ica.

Students of anthropology may find my comments useful on why and how people are important to an ethnographer and how a field project is a tissue of personal relationships. My main interest as a graduate student was in the ethnography of the Balkans, but when political events there made fieldwork unlikely, I turned to Peru, where I already had an interest in archaeology. Because my interest in Peru had originally been archaeological, this strongly inclined me toward a long-range historical view of Peruvian society. I went to Ica rather than to some other place because John Rowe had worked there often and I had done extensive analysis of some of the archaeological collections made in the Ica Valley early in the century by Max Uhle and deposited with the University of California. Thus, my field location, like that of many ethnographers, was established through a series of historical accidents.

Once there, with my wife and two small sons, I leaned heavily on those whom other anthropologists had known. My first telephone call was to Duncan Masson from Lima; through him I came to know his colleagues at Anderson, Clayton and through them the agricultural and business community. Through him, by earlier correspondence, I had already arranged to occupy an absent missionary's tiny house, nestled below an enormous sand dune. With him I repaired an old Model A Ford, cut down as a racing car, which was my transportation for the year. That car, in fact, was my entrée to the people of the valley. For months after it finally started, I was startled, disturbed, and even angered as children lined the roads when I drove by, shouting "Lelo, Lelo!" Lelo is the Peruvian nickname for the movie actor Jerry Lewis, and (perhaps because all *blancos* look alike) the peasants thought I looked like him. With that car as a conversation piece (and sometimes an albatross), I came to know one mechanic after another, and in it I took second place in one of the wildest ten-mile jalopy races through the alleys of Ica City that anyone could remember. I look back with a shudder on the fact that my assistant driver and I ran without helmets, seat belts, or roll bar, but remember with satisfaction the cries of "Go, Lelo, go!" as we lapped the field, and the unanimous approbation when we tipped into a cotton field a driver who had locked axles with us to slow us down. That race was a social solvent, an initiation rite which removed me from the dubious status of student and snoop into one of local celebrity and member of the community, a fluid status from which I could talk to banker and field hand alike. Typhoid and lack of funds had forced my family home, and from the winner of the race and numerous others I found renewed hospitality.

All of this was long before Project Camelot and the debacle of student activities financed by the Central Intelligence Agency. No one thought I was a political spy, but many were convinced I was a tax collector or an industrial espionage agent. Again, that Model A was a wonderful cover, at least in the valley. Beyond it, there was no way to proceed except through personal links. When Ynez Haase and I surveyed 37 fishing villages along 5000 kilometers of coast, we started with Jorge Moquillaza's family in the fisherman's inland base of Comatrana, then to his *compadre* in the fishing camp of Laguna Grande, and then from *compadre* to *compadre*, *padrino* to *ahijado*, for 5000 kilometers. When the links ran out, as they occasionally did, it could be less than pleasant; I can remember being backed against a wall and interrogated by a group of hard-eyed young bucks in Matacaballo (Sechura), who were convinced I was spying out their fishing grounds for a commercial fishery.

Race was a doubled-edged factor in the question of social acceptance. Iquenian society is as race-conscious as our own, but race is used more as a culture- or stratum-identifier than as a social factor in its own right. Being a *blanco* was more important in stereotyping me than being a *norteamericano*. It put me above the peasants, so that they were often honored by my attentions; at the same time, the fact that I hobnobbed with them made it difficult for them to feel resentful of my status — after all, I was not one of *their blancos*. It made it easy to talk with members of the upper class, although they were sometimes shocked by the fact that I *did* hobnob with the peasants. To them, I verged on being a *mataperro* — an old Limeñan term for ne'er-do-well sons of the wealthy who hung around low-class places of ill repute. Members of the middle class, many of whom still could not decide which part of society they really belonged to, but who were desperately eager to belong to a particular part, were just ambivalent. I took a lot of kidding from the middle class, as well as more open hostility. For example, my spoken Spanish was principally acquired in Ica, so that I spoke a distinctly local and peasant dialect (with prevelar [s] as [h], and so on). My speech was thus the cause of much mirth — a *blanco* talking like a *cholo*, rather like a white American speaking English in a Negro dialect.

My own attitudes toward Iquenians were and continue to be ambivalent, and they reflect the rigid class structure of their society in the way I felt about members of different classes. I have never liked the Peruvian petit bourgeois; his Junior Chamber of Commerce ethos, Latin *machismo*, and status strivings appropriate to Peyton Place form a repellent combination. Many members of the old aristocratic families belonged to a grand tradition, which shared many of my own values. The peasants were tough, amiable, and trustworthy; the fishermen, particularly, were frank and likable. Perhaps the most unexpected of my attitudes was my spontaneous liking and trust for the Negroes; I couldn't bring myself to believe that they were really Peruvians, and in some ways, they seemed closer to me than other Iquenians. Enculturation in a caste-stratified society has some strange effects. Only the migrant highlanders were really foreign to me, and the most serious fault in this book is the lack of intimate information on them; I could not bridge the communication gap, and most of my work was carried out in a part of the valley where they are few in number.

It is to all these people, about whom my feelings are so varied, that I owe the most.

E. A. H.

Berkeley
April, 1969

Contents

POWER IN ICA

The Structural History
of a Peruvian Community

CHAPTER ONE

Introduction

Two things strike the observer of Peruvian society with great force. One is the enormous amount of technological, cultural, and social change that has occurred since the fall of the Inca state. The other is the great importance of hierarchical ordering in all aspects of social life and the relative impermeability of boundaries between segments of that hierarchy. Closer examination reveals that major changes in the economic system, in the demographic constitution of the population, in the political system, and in social mobility have gone hand in hand. The problem of Peruvian social history is that of understanding how one relatively rigid social organization can have changed successively into other relatively rigid social organizations.

The analysis is complicated by the fact that Peruvian society has never been and is not now a totally coherent system, characterized by congruence in the differential allocation of resources and ben-

Representatives from both extremes of the social spectrum in Ica: left, *a member of the upper class (see page 65); right, a highlander (see page 103), typical of the lower lower class. The photographs used in the text were taken by the author.*

efits across all sectors. One cannot, in fact, speak of a single structure of Peruvian society but only of several substructures and of their relative correspondence at different points in time. The simplest model that is still adequate portrays three facets of the social structure, three systems of distribution of scarce and valued goods. One of these is the system of distribution of wealth, another that of power, and the third that of prestige. In the conceptual scheme of Max Weber, these are all aspects of the ability of men to "realize their own will in a communal action against the resistance of others who are participating in the action." [1] These systems, or substructures of the total social scheme, are descriptions of the ways in which the bases of social position are distributed among the population. Each system is analytically distinct from the others, although they may overlap in their empirical relationships, and each forms the basis for a different kind of social grouping: the differential distribution of wealth gives rise to *classes*, that of power to *parties*, and that of prestige to *status groups*.[2] Specification of these systems and delineation of the groups based on them depends on identification of the scarce and valued goods pertaining to each — or what the currencies of the systems are. In a money economy or one with property records, it is fairly simple to describe the distribution of wealth. The distribution of power can be identified through the observation of political action and through the nature of legal codes. The distribution of prestige is more difficult to specify, but it depends essentially on native statements of value, on consciousness of social honor, and on observations of style of life. *Methodologically*, prestige is almost a residual category.

The analysis of social change must go further than such descriptive specification of the distribution of valued goods. And it should not be restricted to observations of changing patterns of distribution in each of the substructures, of group or individual mobility along separate dimensions. Rather it must include specification of the interrelationships of the three dimensions, of the degree to which possession of some amount of one social good is

[1] Max Weber 1958. See also Nadel 1951, chapters 6 and 7.
[2] Weber, *op. cit.*

associated with possession of some amount of another social good. With these points in mind, the analysis of social change can be seen to pose several distinct descriptive problems, several foci of observation.

1. Individuals may change their positions in any substructure by gaining or losing the symbols of the substructure but without altering the substructure itself. This is individual mobility.

2. Particular segments of the society may change their positions in any substructure, leaving other segments where they were. This is group mobility and a modification of the structure itself; a convenient example is the rise of the middle class. It is important to note that such a change is not necessarily the same as that described under heading 1, above. Even if all the members of one hierarchical class exchange positions with all the members of another, there has occurred no real structural change, since the upper and lower class positions still exist in the same relationship.

3. The entire society may shift within any substructure by gaining or losing the symbols of that substructure. A general rise in "standard of living" is illustrative of this kind of change. It may also be viewed conversely, as a process in which the symbols of a substructure move through the society in an increasing or decreasing wave.[3]

4. The congruence and relative importance of the three substructures may change; this constitutes a major alteration in the overall social structure. For example, in the European Middle Ages most wealthy men were aristocrats and most aristocrats were wealthy. There was a close "fit" between the extents of the two classes, and the degree of congruence between the substructures of wealth and authority was therefore high. At a later period, some wealthy men were not aristocrats, and some aristocrats were poor. The classes were no longer isomorphic, and the congruence of the substructures of wealth and authority had decreased. Further, noble birth, or the hereditary right to a position of authority, became less important, and possession of wealth became more important in the assessment of overall social status.

[3] Fallers 1954.

4

The data from Ica, as well as from other societies, suggest that some of these changes may be logically interrelated. Our concern in this study, however, is only to describe and analyze the concrete data from Ica according to reasonably well-established methodological principles and to demonstrate that certain kinds of social change have occurred. An abstract or metaphysical analysis of the interrelationships between the varieties of structural change and also an extension of these theoretical principles to comparative data from areas other than Ica are beyond the scope of the study.

The study first presents a brief sketch of the geography, demographic and political history, and ethnography of the valley to orient the reader. Following this sketch are sections dealing with the development of particular aspects of Iquenian life from our earliest records to the present. The data of these sections are, of course, more complete for the present than for the historic or prehistoric past, and some of my remarks on past conditions are necessarily inferential. The completeness of historical coverage also varies according to the body of material considered; it is better for such matters as agriculture than for many considerations of social class. Treatment of these materials is not wholly descriptive but includes comments on the pertinence of the data to the general thesis of social change. The descriptive materials have often been selected to illustrate such change merely by their inclusion or juxtaposition in the text.

In the final chapter, the description of life in Ica is rephrased in terms of the theoretical framework given above, and the substructures of wealth, authority, and prestige are examined at different points in history. These remarks on structural process are concluded by an examination of the congruence of the three substructures through time and by an evaluation of the coherence of the total social scheme.

CHAPTER TWO

General
Description

The Ica Valley lies on the arid southern coast of Peru about 300 kilometers south of Lima (Map I). Like most Peruvian coastal valleys, it contains an intermittent river which flows between January and April in years of sufficient rainfall in the Andes. It is unusual among the coastal rivers, however, in that it flows from north to south for much of its length, instead of running directly westward from the Andes to the sea. This study deals with that portion of the valley between and including the Haciendas Huamaní and Ocucaje, an area which is about ninety kilometers long and varies in width between two and fifteen kilometers (Map II). The rest of the valley is only sparsely inhabited.

The valley, like most of the Peruvian coast, is extremely dry. Aside from a few drizzles in the middle of the summer (December to March), which may total a half-inch of precipitation, and

6

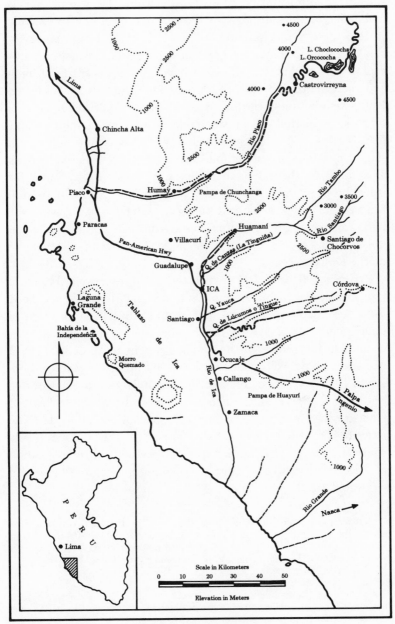

Map I.   The Ica Valley.

7

the heavy morning mists (*garuas*) of the winter, the seasonal floods and underground water flow are the only sources of moisture.[1] Only in rare years is precipitation sufficient to support any grasses or shrubs, although some cacti grow on slopes above 700 meters. However, before this century during which intensified cotton farming and the canalization of the river extended the area of cultivated land, ground water in the low-lying areas of the south valley as far as Ocucaje supported an impenetrable growth of mesquite, cane, reed, shrubs, and tough grasses. Many low spots were filled with stagnant water the year round, but most of these have dried up as a result of the extensive pumping of underground water for irrigation during the last decade. The crucial element in the fertility of the valley is water. Controlled water for irrigation — the right amount at the right time, on agricultural land instead of in salty marshes — has always been the key to human achievement on the Peruvian coast.

Between 1907 and 1935, when deep irrigation wells began to tap the supplies of underground water, it appeared that the hope for a dependable source had been realized. But the utilization of underground water was so rapid and extensive that the supply, which had taken eons in the building, began to be depleted in a few years. Some wells which yielded 1800 gallons of water a minute in 1952 have dried to a trickle. Attempts were made to bring water from other sources, such as the Pisco River or the lakes of Choclococha and Orcococha just over the continental divide.[2] The latter project, which began at the turn of the century, was finally completed in 1959.[3] It has led to major revisions in the regulation of irrigation, shifts in agricultural technology, and an expansion of cultivated area.[4]

---

[1] Of forty-one rivers on the coast of Peru in 1956, the Ica was one of four which dried completely at some time during the year; it was dry from about March to December. For general geographical descriptions see Preusse-Sperber 1913; Romero 1939; Schweigger 1947; and sources in Hammel 1962a.

[2] González Herrera n.d.: 257–296; Sutton 1905.

[3] *La Prensa*, Lima, November 20, 1959.

[4] I have not been able to obtain specific information on these changes, beyond the data already reported in this book and based on the 1957–1958 field session. National statistics are too gross; for example, they seldom give the amount of cultivated land and crop yield for the valley itself, usually combin-

8

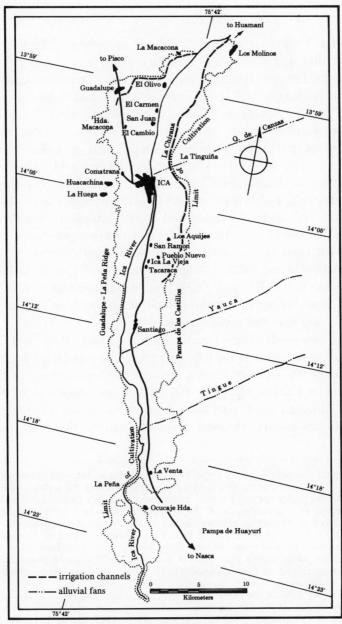

Map II. *The Huamaní–Ocucaje Zone.*

9

The Ica Valley was probably inhabited as early as 2500 B.C. by preceramic agriculturists and fishermen living near the mouth of the river. For four thousand years there was a steady elaboration of native culture and social structure. The simple fishing and farming culture of the preceramic period, with its minimal crops of cotton, peanuts, squash, and gourds, was enriched by the introduction of pottery and additional crops, such as maize, about 1500 B.C. The remarkable artistic styles of Chavinoid type came into the area about 800 B.C., probably as a manifestation of a new religious cult. Full-fledged urban life made its appearance about 200 B.C. Tiahuanacoid religious and artistic influences made themselves felt about A.D. 800, and Inca civilization penetrated the southern coast in the latter half of the fifteenth century.[5] The population of the valley in late aboriginal times appears to have been between 25,000 and 39,000, and habitation sites were scattered from the upper canyon at least as far south as Zamaca, a greater area than that occupied today.

The Spaniards under Pizarro, having invaded Peru in 1532, pushed as far as Ica in the following year. The population became subject to the Spanish Crown, through the intermediacy of the officers of Pizarro who were the original *encomenderos* of the area. Although the Crown made legal efforts to protect the aboriginal inhabitants, historical accounts indicate that they were

---

ing figures for both Ica and Palpa or Ica-Palpa-Nasca. Informal information suggests, however, that the dearth of water is as bad as ever (or perhaps worse), because the water needed for land newly brought under cultivation has left no surplus for replenishment of the depleted underground water table. Expansion of cultivation is reflected indirectly in the phenomenal growth of population in the southern part of the valley, where the effect of new water for expanded cultivation would have been the strongest. It is ironic that the increase in water supply came just at a time when the profit from cotton cultivation is said to have declined (J. H. Rowe, personal communication, based on comments by R. A. Rawlins).

[5] Lanning 1967 is the most recent source. See also Engel 1957; Hammel, Norsworthy and Rowe MS; Lanning MS; Lanning and Hammel 1961; Menzel MS, 1958, 1959; Rowe 1946, 1947, 1958a, 1958b, 1963; Strong 1957; Willey 1958.

ruthlessly exploited.[6] From 80 to 90 percent of the Indians fled, died of disease or malnutrition, or were killed during the following century, and they were partly replaced by wholesale importation of Negro slaves. The total population of the valley just after the conquest, including the newcomers, was only a third or a half of the preconquest population, and even by the end of the eighteenth century there were only about 15,000 inhabitants. With Indian serfs, Negro slaves, and later Asiatic bond servants as a base, the Europeans established an economic, social, and political overlordship that has lasted to the present. The revolution against Spain in 1820–1824 led to some reshuffling of political and economic position among them but did not affect their supremacy over the native population and the imported Africans and Asiatics. The War of the Pacific and the Chilean occupation of Ica in the 1880's had equally little effect on their position.

The population of the valley began to recover from its colonial experiences and almost achieved its preconquest size toward the end of the nineteenth century, when numbers increased to about 24,000. By the middle of the twentieth century, modern transportation and communication, heavy industry and commercial agriculture had brought Ica face to face with the rest of the world as she had never been before. The technological changes that have occurred in the last generation are in many ways more extensive than any that have come to Ica previously, and the rate of change continues to accelerate. At the same time, the breakdown of the old colonial social scheme, which began in 1820 and is now reaching its climax, has drastically changed the nonmaterial aspects of life in Ica.[7] A marked feature of all these changes has been the demographic developments. The population of the valley stands at about four times its aboriginal size (102,000), and most of that growth has been concentrated in the city of Ica and in the larger rural towns.[8]

[6] See Kubler 1952; Perú MS; Prado 1941; Rowe 1953, 1957.

[7] For further details see Caso 1950; Donaire Vizarreta 1941; Hammel 1959; Miró Quesada Sosa 1947; Paulette 1953; Rossel Castro 1954; Wellin MS; and other items cited in the text.

[8] Peru, 1961 Census of Population. From 1940 to 1961, the population of Ica City rose from 20,896 to 62,429, an increase of 199 percent or practically

11

The Pan-American Highway enters the Ica Valley between the town of Guadalupe and the village of El Olivo, passing through a gap in the chain of hills which forms its northern and western limit. The verdant foliage of the valley is a marked change from the barren desert which lies between Ica and Pisco to the north. The land around this entrance to the valley is flat and occupied by cotton fields belonging to wealthy *hacendados*. To the left of the entrance, in a great sweep from north to south, lie the barren crags of the Andes, towering to 5000 meters high in the space of 60 kilometers; to the right is the rock rampart of the Guadalupe-La Peña ridge, rising about 300 meters above the valley floor.

Looking up the throat of the Ica canyon, one can see almost to the borders of the Hacienda Huamaní; here, too, most of the land is composed of large cotton fields. East of the river the situation is similar, but that area includes the patchwork fields of small farmers who grow a variety of food crops and fruits. Eleven kilometers to the south lies the city of Ica, still of rural aspect on its northern border where phenomenal urban growth of recent years has engulfed the village of San Joaquin.

The city itself has a modern appearance only for a block or so around the plaza, and even there the past shows itself in the crumbling remains of a few ornate colonial doorways. Outside the central area the buildings are almost all one story high and made of adobe or wattle-and-daub. It is in this less modern area that the principal market of the city is found — a great barnlike structure, covering half a city block and crowded with the tiny stalls of a multitude of food vendors. In the narrow alley back of the market other vendors sell pots and pans, clothing, and some prepared foods. Here, too, are the shaded enclosures of a few highland

---

a tripling in size, while the number of persons living in rural towns and villages rose from 33,259 to 39,671, an increase of only 16 percent. The degree of increasing urbanization is greater than that indicated here, because persons living in rural towns are counted as "rural." The Peruvian census of 1940 classified as urban all those centers of population which were capitals of districts, provinces, or departments, as well as all others whose population exceeded the mean population of such capitals. By this standard, the population of the valley was 49 percent urban in 1940 and 58 percent urban in 1961.

women who sell crude pottery, wooden spoons, and a myriad of herbal remedies from the Andean plateau and the jungle beyond.

Farther to the south is a secondary plaza, and beyond it the residential area of Luren in which most of the wealthier inhabitants of the city live. The neat lawns and trimly decorated bungalows, apartment houses, and duplexes present a strong contrast with the poorer parts of the city. The tidy homes of Luren are only a stone's throw from the squalor of the river bank, crowded with the mud-plastered and adobe houses which some wealthy men of the city rent to the poor. Half-naked children play noisily in the filth, and the dry bed of the river serves as a community latrine.

Beyond the city lies another expanse of large cotton fields. To the left, across the great irrigation ditch of the Chirana, rise the alluvial fans of the ravines of La Tinguiña, Yauca, and Tingue and the massif of the Andes. At the edge of the fans is another enclave of small farmers, cultivating their checkerboard fields in traditional fashion and occasionally planting crops on the fans themselves when a flash flood from the mountains provides water for irrigation. The areas of smallholders are unique on the Peruvian coast except for a similar but smaller enclave in Chincha, and they contrast strongly with the lands of wealthy owners. The signs of modern agriculture such as pumphouses are rare. The ground, instead of being flat and furrowed, is excavated into a pattern of square, flat-bottomed irrigation basins (*pozas*) perhaps ten meters square and a meter deep. In the floors of these *pozas* some cotton may be grown, but always with an abundance of food crops, such as maize, lima beans, sweet potatoes, or peas. Around the borders of the pits grows a bewildering variety of fruit trees and grapevines.

The settlements in these peasant areas are often line villages, but the older ones are usually arranged around a central plaza, after the old colonial pattern. Here, too, the contrast of old and new is striking. Houses patterned after those of nineteenth-century haciendas stand next to some modelled on a Limeñan style of the 1930's and next to some others of a type found abundantly in archaeological deposits. A colonial church is cheek-by-jowl with a modern metal water tank, and an occasional pickup truck weaves its way through a traffic of creaking country busses and donkeys with their barefoot keepers.

13

CHAPTER THREE

Agriculture
and Husbandry

<small>THE PRECONQUEST PERIOD</small> (<small>TO</small> 1533)

The roster of cultivated plants known to the American Indians was a long one, and the Indians of the Ica Valley and adjacent areas of the Peruvian coast raised a wide variety of them. Archaeological excavations in the dry desert fringes of the valley have unearthed the actual remains and also drawings on ceramic vessels of maize, peanuts, sweet manioc (*yuca*), the sweet root of *achira*, tuber beans (*jíquima*), lima beans (named after the capital city of Lima), jack beans, cotton, squash, and gourds. Some trees with edible fruit were probably also planted or at least cared for and irrigated: *lúcuma* (which today flavors a delicious ice cream), avocado, and *pacay* (which has a fruit like a very large mesquite bean). The earliest agriculture presents a strange forecast of modern concentration on industrial crops such as cotton, since the

<small>14</small>

oldest agricultural sites in Peru contain only cotton, gourds, and squash, the first two crops having been used for fishing lines and floats.[1] Remains of domestic animals in the archaeological sites of any period are less abundant, and dogs, guinea pigs, and llamas were probably the only species.

The physical environment seems to have been more varied in the preconquest period. Wild species of plants and animals were more abundant, and water, in particular, seems to have been more evenly distributed as a consequence of less intensive cultivation. The area cultivated extended further than it does today, stretching from the narrow gorge of the upper river as far south as Zamaca, instead of terminating effectively at Ocucaje.

THE COLONIAL PERIOD (1533-1820)

The Spaniards effected revolutionary changes in the kinds of crops and domestic animals, as well as in the techniques of cultivation. Some new crops were introduced from Europe or Africa, and some were brought from other areas by the Spaniards or perhaps by the Incas.[2] The cultivated plants in Ica in the late sixteenth and early seventeenth centuries, in addition to those cited for the preconquest period, were as follows: wheat, alfalfa, chick-pea, melon, grape, blackberry (*mora*), cherry (*guinda*), fig, apple, quince, pomegranate, melon pear (*pepino*), hot pepper, sugarcane, cabbage, eggplant, and possibly coconut, coca, and the date.[3] The animals introduced by the Spaniards included the horse, donkey (and thus the mule), cattle, sheep, goats, and swine.[4] European techniques of plowing and caring for the grapevine were introduced at the same time.

Early Spanish accounts give some indication of what agriculture was like in those days; they praise the fertility of the soil but deplore the lack of water. All the early travellers were impressed by the quality of the vineyards in Ica. There were vines in Ica by

---

[1] See Dawson MS; Lanning 1967; Zeuner 1963:436-439.
[2] See Cobo 1956; Valdizán and Maldonado 1922, Vol. 2; Weberbauer 1945.
[3] See Anonymous MS; Foster 1960:50-69; Sánchez Elías 1957:48-50; Vásquez de Espinosa 1948:449-452.
[4] See Foster 1960:70-76.

1553, almost immediately after the introduction of the grape to Peru (ca. 1551), and within fifty years Ica was one of the principal vineyard areas in all the Indies. Vine cultivation was adopted by independent Indian farmers as early as the 1590's.[5]

The distribution of agricultural land in the colonial period was one of great plantations existing side by side with tiny plots. The original extension of the Hacienda Huamaní, for example, was about 2100 hectares of cultivated land with thirty times as much uncultivated mountain terrain in addition, totalling almost forty square miles. Some of the principal Indians (*caciques*) of the valley owned plots of land as large as 180 hectares, but the majority of Indian plots were smaller, just as peasant properties are today.[6] Agricultural labor on the large haciendas was provided by Negro slaves. Sharecropping may have been carried on by landless Indians (*yanaconas*), but there is only linguistic evidence for the practice.[7]

THE REPUBLICAN AND EARLY MODERN PERIOD
(1820–1900)

The general agricultural patterns established at the conquest continued in effect until almost the beginning of this century. The major change in agriculture was the introduction of commercial cotton growing by a wealthy planter, Ismael Elías, in 1844. As in other areas of Peru, cotton became a popular crop under the scarcity conditions created by the American Civil War, but it de-

[5] Sánchez Elías 1957.

[6] Anicama MS. The total amount of land cultivated about 1639 was approximately 16,000 hectares (1 hectare = 2.47 acres). There were probably about 1.14 hectares of land per capita of total population and about 16–20 hectares of land per owner. The last figure is the arithmetic mean; in view of the skewed distribution of ownership, most farmers had much less than that.

[7] The word *yanacona* in modern Peruvian Spanish means "sharecropper," although other terms are more commonly used to designate that role in Ica, cf. Castro Pozo 1947 (e.g., *partidario*). There were many *yanaconas* in colonial Ica, identified as landless Indians from other areas who performed personal services for the Spaniards and who were exempt from payment of tribute. No specific mention is made of sharecropping in colonial sources. It is conceivable, however, that the *yanaconas* served as foremen for the Negro slaves, a reversal of the current practice in which Negroes often serve as foremen for migrant Indian labor from the sierra.

16

clined toward the end of the century. Most cotton was grown on large estates, often by sharecroppers, while small, independent farmers continued to have grapes as their principal cash crop. Sugarcane and rice, the other great commercial crops of Peru, were never cultivated in Ica on a large scale, although some experimental plantings were made.[8] The most common use of sugarcane in the colonial and republican periods was to make *aguardiente*, and for this the grape was preferred in Ica. Further, sugarcane and rice require much more water than the vine, so that the latter was a more practical crop in the arid Ica Valley.

By 1900 about 17,000 hectares were under cultivation, providing roughly 0.5 hectares per capita of total population. Between two-thirds and three-fourths of the land was in the hands of large owners.

The character of the labor situation changed markedly in republican times. All slaves were freed in 1855, and large landowners were forced to look elsewhere for a source of labor. Some haciendas on the south coast are said to have ceased operations when cheap slave labor was no longer available. In part, slaves were replaced by Chinese and Polynesian bond servants, although Asiatic immigration to Ica was much less extensive than it was to other areas of Peru[9] and came to an end about 1875. The practice of sharecropping probably received considerable impetus from the shortage of labor brought about by emancipation of the slaves and by cessation of the Asiatic traffic. The first record of sharecropping dates from 1885 and indicates an extensive pattern of owner-cropper arrangements, although the details of the contracts are not reported.[10] It is further possible that the number of migrant laborers descending from the sierra to the coast increased about 1875–1885 to fill the cheap labor market vacated by the slaves and bond servants; the first report of highland laborers is in 1905.[11]

---

[8] Occasional published data on cane production in "Ica" refer not to the valley but to the Department of Ica. Some cane is grown in the Chincha Valley, for example. See Castelnau 1851; *Peru Today* 1912.

[9] Stewart 1951.

[10] González Herrera n.d.:224 ff.

[11] Chabert and Dubosc 1908.

Crops. The principal commercial crops at the beginning of the century were grapes, cotton, figs, a variety of vegetables, watermelons, and alfalfa, in that order.[12] By 1905 cotton was beginning to replace grapes as a cash crop, and the first vineyards were torn out to make room for cotton fields.[13] Cotton was preferred to grapes because it was not subject to the high taxes on alcohol (the usual end product of the grapes), because it required only a tenth of the field labor per unit area, and because the grower could obtain ready financing on a high percentage of his expected crop. Obviously, these are advantages only to commercial growers, so that the replacement of grapes by cotton began among and was for a long time confined to wealthy agriculturists.

Cotton production increased rapidly during World War I but fell sharply in the depression of 1929, so that many farmers became bankrupt. Recovery was quick, however, and production continued to increase, until today it stands at about ten times its previous high point during World War I.

Grape production declined sharply until 1945, when the area devoted to vines stabilized at about 5 percent of the area cultivated. Many more varieties of grapes are produced than in the colonial and republican periods, and production efficiency has doubled since 1900. The owners of the modernized wineries, who are now almost the only large-scale growers of grapes, have imported over sixty types of grapes in an attempt to produce fine table and sweet wines and champagnes. In recent years the practice of replacing grapevines with cotton has been adopted by owners of medium-sized plots, so that the vineyards still existing are owned either by the large wineries or by a multitude of small-scale farmers.

Today the valley produces an imposing variety of food crops, culinary and medicinal herbs, but in quantities less than it consumes. Most of its land is cultivated in cotton or in grapes (used for wine and brandy), and great amounts of food are imported

[12] Sutton 1905.
[13] *Peru Today* 1912.

Three views of the Ica Valley showing agricultural crops: top, *an alfalfa patch at the desert's edge, looking toward the Andes;* middle, *workers cleaning cotton, the chief crop;* bottom, *a vineyard.*

from Lima and neighboring valleys such as Chincha and Ingenio which raise some surplus food. Almost all the food grown locally comes from the small farms.[14]

Land Distribution. Although final evaluation of the statistics of land distribution is a detailed and complicated process, some of the general outlines of the history of wealth in land are clear. The distribution of cultivated land is still similar to the pattern of the colonial period: Latifundia coexist with minifundia, a feature characteristic of the Ica and Chincha valleys but rare elsewhere in coastal Peru, where almost all properties are quite large. In Ica, a few persons own vast amounts of land, while a larger number of persons hold a small amount. The amount of cultivated land per capita of total population has fluctuated as the amounts of land and of people have changed; the per capita share fell gradually from 1617 until about 1912, as the population grew but the

[14] Precise data are not available for the valley itself, but the 1961 agro-economic census gives figures for the Department of Ica on percentage of cultivated area devoted to various crops and on crop yields. The Department of Ica contained about 81,000 hectares of cultivated land, with the following percentages devoted to major crops (contrasting figures are given for Peru as a whole):

	Cotton	Maize	Pota-toes	Barley	Wheat	Cane	Rice	Grape
Ica	90%	5%	<1%	<1%	<1%	<1%	<1%	ca. 4%
Peru	13%	18%	10%	9%	8%	4%	4%	0.3%

A similar picture of the overwhelming attention to cotton can be obtained from the following figures, in which the tonnage of each crop is given as a percentage of the total tonnage of all crops listed for the Department of Ica in the 1961 census: rice 0.07%, achira and cañihua <0.01%, oats <0.01%, barley 0.65%, maize 3.72%, quinoa 0.0%, wheat 0.24%, peas 0.04%, beans 1.51%, chick-peas 0.15%, broad beans 0.25%, lima beans 1.25%, sweet potatoes 0.79%, sweet manioc 0.21%, cotton 91.09%. Grapes are not listed in the census tables, but they would probably rank second in tonnage. With the exception of maize, lima beans, and the common bean, most of the food crops listed above were probably grown either in Nasca and Palpa or on the higher Andean slopes out of the valley. In 1957, to my knowledge, only one hacienda in the Ica Valley grew any food crops whatever, and it had devoted a small area to an experimental planting of common beans. Maize *was* grown by cotton farmers, but only as a subterfuge to accommodate Peruvian law on the required percentage of land to be devoted to food crops; the maize was planted, allowed to shade the young cotton plants, and then cut down long before it could be harvested. (For source data, see the 1961 *Primer Censo Nacional Agropecuario*, p. XIV, Tables 21–23.)

amount of land remained constant. When cotton was introduced, much new land was put under cultivation, so the per capita share rose again. When the population expanded, the per capita share diminished again between 1918 and the 1940's, but the irrigation of the Pampa de los Castillos in the 1950's brought the per capita share back to almost the 1918 level. Since most of the population growth has been urban, the share of land per farmer has not fluctuated as widely. It fell steadily after 1617, rising slightly after irrigation of the Pampa de los Castillos; similarly, the ratio of farmers is less, about a sixth of the 1617 ratio of farmers to total population.

The distribution of land between large owners and small owners changed markedly between 1905 and 1957.[15] In 1905 large owners held 2.6 times as much cultivated land as small farmers; in 1918 they held 5.8 times as much and in 1957 held about 5.0 times as much as the small owners. The reason for this change from a

[15] A large owner in Ica, in traditional tax usage, is one who owns more than six hectares. The land distribution on the floor of the valley in 1957 was as follows: the modal holding was from a quarter to a third of a hectare, the mean was 3.4 hectares, and the range from infinitesimal plots of a thirtieth of a hectare (about 60 feet on a side) to domains of 1800 hectares of valuable cotton land. There was about one hectare of land for every three inhabitants of the valley, and about one farmer for every ten inhabitants. Five-sixths of the land was in the hands of large owners. Irrigation of the Pampa de los Castillos on the Yauca fan, by the use of deep wells in the 1950's, added about 4500 hectares, bringing the total amount of cultivated land in the valley to about 27,000 hectares. Precise data on the distribution of land on the Pampa were not available, but the effect of the additional land was to increase the average amount of land per capita of total population to about half a hectare and the share per farmer to about 4 hectares. Similarly, there are no data available on the amount of cultivated land added after 1959 through the completion of the new aqueduct from Choclococha, although the intention was to add 69,000 new acres and provide additional water for 57,000 already under cultivation (U.S. Department of the Army 1965:459). Data in the 1961 agricultural census do not separate the Ica Valley from the rest of the Department, so that the figures are not directly comparable, even for relative distributions, because there are many fewer small farmers in the Palpa-Nasca area than in Ica. Nevertheless, the data for the Department are interesting. Of about 7500 owners, 73 percent held less than 5 hectares each and together accounted for only 4 percent of the approximately 150,000 hectares given in the census. Conversely, 96 percent of the land was in the hands of the 27 percent of the population which owned more than 5 hectares. The 1961 census data unfortunately do not divide at the traditional point of 6 hectares, so that comparison is again impeded. For comparative information see Ford 1955.

slightly skewed distribution around the turn of the century to a more sharply skewed one at mid-century lies in the method by which cotton cultivation expanded. Most of the land utilized in the expansion was in the form of fallow areas, mesquite thickets, sandy patches, or salt-grass swamps, which were held by large haciendas in huge tracts, but used only for pasture, if at all. When modern techniques and the high investment returns of cotton cultivation made expansion into these areas possible, it was the large owners who developed or bought them. Thus, although the whole valley was expanding agriculturally, the large owners were expanding their holdings twice as fast as the small owners, because the means for expansion (cash for capital investment, as well as good social standing and large holdings as collateral, serving as a basis for credit) were already in their possession. The differential in rate of expansion created a wider gap in the distribution of wealth.

Agricultural Labor. In the early part of this century, before the commercial cultivation of cotton became popular, permanent agricultural labor on large haciendas was provided by sharecroppers. In peak seasons the labor force was augmented by wage laborers from the ranks of the small peasants and migrant *serranos*.[16] The details of the sharecropping contracts varied widely, but in general the system was as follows: Large landowners entered into sharecropping contracts to assure themselves of a steady labor supply, particularly for the vines which require a great amount of hand labor. Peasants with insufficient or no land became sharecroppers in order to obtain steady employment and a plot of ground on which to cultivate their food. The landowner in these circumstances was known as the *hacendado* and the sharecropper as a *partidario* (the term *yanacona* was seldom used). Sometimes two peasants would combine their resources and work a plot of ground in partnership (*compañía*). The *compañía* relationship was one between social equals, as the term itself indicates. The *hacendado-partidario* relationship was one of master and indentured servant or serf.

[16] Chabert and Dubosc 1908. See Adams 1964 for a review of rural labor in Latin America, and Mintz 1953 on the special nature of the rural proletariat.

22

In a standard sharecropping contract, an *hacendado* growing food crops provided land, water rights, seed, and oxen (sometimes the plow as well) to the *partidario*. The latter performed all the labor and in addition was obliged to work one or two days per week for the owner without pay, at a fraction of the regular wage, or more rarely at the regular wage. He also worked for the hacienda for wages on other days when labor was needed. Usually he and his family were forbidden to work for anyone else for wages. The crop was apportioned evenly between the *hacendado* and the *partidario*, either by dividing the sacks of produce or by cropping alternate rows or plots. Grapes were never grown under such an arrangement but were cultivated by wage labor or by *partidarios* on their days of obligatory labor for the exclusive benefit of the owner. The ground beneath the vines, however, was usually planted to food crops and sharecropped as indicated. In a variant arrangement, the owner rented land to the *partidario* at a fixed number of days of labor per unit of area. The restrictions on the mobility and freedom of action of the sharecropper are strikingly similar to the constraints placed on serfs in medieval Europe. This kind of labor contract uses the owner's supply and control of land to assure him of labor in peak seasons, and it allows the peasant, whose only resource is his labor, to trade that for some security of tenure. Sharecropping rights were passed from father to son; it was difficult to get rid of a sharecropper, and sharecroppers had first rights of claim on an owner's assets should he be bankrupted.

As commercial cotton cultivation was extended throughout the valley, it was subsumed under the system for food crops and was worked by sharecroppers. Usually a sharecropper surrendered his entire crop to the owner, who sold it together with the other cotton produced on the hacienda. The sharecropper received half the sale price for the cotton he delivered, minus a 10 to 20 percent deduction for handling and transportation.

Between 1910 and 1945 several reforms introduced by national legislation, which guaranteed certain rights of tenant farmers, made sharecropping unprofitable for the farmer and risky for his creditors. As a result, the large commercial cotton companies which financed much of the cotton farming refused to advance money to owners with sharecroppers on their land. Since almost all commercial growers financed their operations on cash advances from the contracted buyer, they immediately took steps to eliminate sharecropping even though it was illegal to do so under those same reforms. Additional factors in this decision were that increased mechanization and the general shift from grape to cotton cultivation had lessened the need for a large permanent labor force. Further, sharecropping was recognized as an inefficient system when crops of high market value had to be produced by modern methods, since supervision of the labor force in the sharecropping system was inadequate. Within a few years, sharecropping had effectively disappeared from the large haciendas, although a few favored "old servants" still retain their plots. Some sharecroppers were allowed to become standing-renters (e.g., in Ocucaje) and to continue paying for the use of the land with a share of their cotton crop, sold via the hacienda at a 10 percent discount. Some sharecropping of the *compañía* type still exists on medium-sized properties which grow grapes, i.e., for the food crops under the vines.

As sharecropping decreased it was no longer as easy for absentee owners to derive their income from their lands; cash renters were harder to find than sharecroppers. Consequently, a much greater proportion of the large properties are now worked under the direct supervision of the owners or through the agency of professional administrators responsible to them. Other lands are rented on a cash or standing-rent basis to one or more renters. The increased opportunities for renting have also stimulated partnerships among the small peasants; they more frequently pool their labor and cash resources to work a rented plot than formerly.[17]

Labor Exchange. The traditional sharecropping arrangements

[17] The 1961 agricultural census indicates that in the Ica-Palpa zone, 12 percent of the properties under 5 hectares and 23 percent of those over 5 hectares in size were rented, while 7 percent of those under 5 hectares and 5 percent of those over were held under some sharecropping arrangement (*aparcería* or *yanaconaje*). Renting (either standing-rent or cash rent) is thus more frequent on large properties, while the older sharing methods are more common on small properties. Altogether, 47 percent of the cultivated land area was rented, while only 3 percent was in some other sharing arrangement. The miscellaneous and mixed categories of the census are not included in these percentages.

24

were common on large and medium properties which yielded enough crop to support more than one family, but small owners worked their lands with family labor and with that of their friends, in a system of cooperative labor exchange called *torna*. Many of the major agricultural tasks of the year, such as field clearing, plowing, threshing, pruning, and grape pressing, were performed under the *torna* system. Irrigation was usually done by the owner and his family alone because the duration of the floods was often so short that all farmers were busy irrigating their fields simultaneously.[18] *Torna* labor was most frequently done on Sundays, when even those small peasants who worked as laborers on haciendas were free to help. The owner of the land was expected to provide drink and often food for the members of the work party and to reciprocate with his own labor when his friends required help on their lands.

Cooperative labor exchange is seldom practiced now in the Ica countryside. The farmers say that most men would prefer to work for pay rather than enter into a tacitly reciprocal contract. Further, the owners of plots would rather hire a diligent workman and get the job done quickly than provide expensive entertainment for friends "who are already too drunk to work." It is difficult to make the same clear distinction between "festive" and "reciprocal" labor that Erasmus does; both characteristics seem to have been combined in Ica. Indeed, it is useful to include sharecropping and corvée labor as forms of symbiotic exchange that decline in frequency under a cash economy.

Agricultural Techniques: Implements. The oxen and Castilian plow introduced by the Spaniards went out of use by 1940, but many small plots, particularly those with grapevines, continue to be cultivated in a still more primitive manner — with the spade alone. Open plots smaller than half a hectare are usually plowed with horse or mule and a mouldboard plow; larger plots are sometimes worked with an animal, but more often with a tractor. Sometimes several small peasants will rent a tractor together to plow their adjacent lands, but that system is only practicable when

18 See Erasmus MS, 1956.

they have open fields, not *pozas,* and are plowing in furrows (see the section on irrigation, below).

On large properties the amount of mechanization is impressive. Plowing, of course, is done with a tractor and various other modern implements, such as multi-blade cultivators and disc harrows. Land is often levelled with modern scoops, drags, and earth movers, and some planting, fertilizing, and fumigating are done by machine. Large cotton fields are sprayed by airplanes where the terrain permits their use. All harvesting is done by hand, since the varieties of cotton grown do not permit mechanical picking. Pruning and the eventual removal of plants from the field are also done by hand, although there have been recent experiments with mechanical cutters and wood-chippers in attempts to mechanize these tasks as well. Most larger farmers would prefer to mechanize all their operations so that they could employ a small but highly skilled labor force and have only a minimum of unskilled field labor,[19] even during peak seasons of labor demand, such as pruning, weeding, and picking.

Agricultural Techniques: Irrigation. The first adequate reports of irrigation techniques date from the early 1900's.[20] It seems reasonable to assume, on the basis of other continuities in the agricultural field, that techniques of irrigation about 1900 were the traditional ones for the valley and had their beginnings in colonial or earlier times. The social regulation of irrigation was reformed at least twice, about 1800 [21] and 1920.[22]

The valley is crisscrossed by a network of named irrigation ditches (*acequias*) which carry the flood waters to the fields. The largest of these is the Chirana (alt. Achirana) which splits off from the river a short distance below the Hacienda Huamaní and

[19] Nevertheless, one *hacendado* strove for more efficient cotton spraying by hiring a large crew of men armed with "Flit" guns, but he was a former Texan, and this was an experiment. In general, and because of the large number of small peasant properties, Ica uses more human muscle than the average for Peru.

[20] Chabert and Dubosc 1908; Gago 1919; Sutton 1907.

[21] According to a document seen by J. H. Rowe in the archive of Alberto Casavilca, Los Aquijes, Ica.

[22] Castro Bulnes MS; Gago 1919; Perú, Ministerio de Fomento, Dirección de las Aguas del Río Ica, MS.

runs some 25 kilometers along the eastern side of the valley. Another large ditch, the Macacona, is an old overflow channel of the Ica River and runs from a point just south of the mouth of the Chirana along the western side of the valley, closer to the Guadalupe–La Peña ridge than the river does now. Hundreds of other ditches fan out from the large ones.

The summer floods seldom come in sufficient quantity to irrigate the entire valley simultaneously; if they did, they would inundate it, since the water comes as a series of flash floods of short duration. Only in years of abundant rain in the sierra is there water in the river for more than a few days at a time. The great ditch of the Chirana has traditional rights to all the water it can hold for the first three months of river flow; if there is any excess during that period, it is allowed to flow on down the river. On any ditch, an irrigator is entitled to block the channel and take as much water as his feeder ditches can hold; this is known as the right of *cabecera*. The Chirana, for example, is "in *cabecera*" of all the river lands which take water from points below its inlet and has its traditional rights for that reason. Because of the *cabecera* system, lands lower on any ditch receive less water in years of scarcity and are consequently less valuable than higher lands, although owners can petition the government irrigation office for additional water (either as *agua de mandamiento* or as *mita* — see below). The relationship between position on a ditch and value is illustrated by the fact that the large landholdings of wealthy owners tend to cluster about the upper ends of ditches, and that the size of holdings diminishes as one proceeds down any ditch.

In addition, major ditches are usually divided into an upper section of *blancos* (whites) and a lower one of *indígenas* (natives). The "whites" usually irrigate between sunrise and sunset on weekdays while the "natives" irrigate at night and on Sundays. It is doubly inconvenient to irrigate at night, not only because of the hour but also because guards must always be sent upstream at night to prevent stealing of irrigation water through higher inlets. Further, the daytime irrigation by "whites" (large owners) tallies with the periods when they have field hands available, while the nights-and-Sundays irrigation of the "natives" tallies with the periods when they are free to work their own lands, since many also work as wage laborers. The geographic distinction on the ditches between "whites" and "natives" is no longer strictly valid, for many large owners now have farms in areas which are traditionally irrigated on nights and Sundays. They usually irrigate with wells to avoid the trouble and expense of sending guards upstream to watch the intervening inlets. Before 1920 there was a great deal of water stealing on the Chirana by large owners who were supposed to irrigate by day but who were low on the ditch in the daytime section. They received insufficient water during the day and simply stole it at night while the "natives" were supposed to be irrigating.[23] The terminological distinction between "whites" and "natives" clearly reflects the Spaniards' arrogation of the more valuable lands during the colonial era.[24] The "reforms" effected in 1920–21 were designed to eliminate water stealing, but they also conveniently coincided with the point in agricultural history at which maximum utilization of water by expanding cotton haciendas became crucial; they favored such haciendas at the expense of the small-holders.

The orderly regulation of irrigation practices implied above is a relatively recent phenomenon, even if the theoretical rights of the Chirana, of *mandamiento* (extra water) and of *mita* (irrigating by turns), are old. Before the establishment of the Comisión Técnica about 1918, the arrangement of irrigation rights was a perfect example of political intrigue, chicanery, and the use of force and influence to attain desired ends — in short, Spanish *caciquismo* was at work. Gago's description (1919) is an outstanding contemporary report on the matter; he was a keen social observer as well as a civil engineer. His observations and recommendations led to the establishment of central governmental control over the irrigation system. While that centralization of control eliminated much of the intrigue on the local, "feeder-ditch" level, it did not do away with it altogether, particularly in local associations of irrigators. Political influence is still important in the ap-

[23] Castro Bulnes MS; Gago 1919; Perú, Ministerio de Fomento, Dirección de las Aguas del Río Ica, MS.
[24] Gago 1919.

28

pointment of the officials of the Comisión, and wealthy landowners sometimes exercise their power to assure the appointment of an engineer who will favor their often shady activities. Even that influence is different from the earlier, local variety, since it is usually channelled through the national government in Lima by men who are powerful both in Ica and in the capital.

About 1900 some attempts were made on large properties to tap underground water for irrigation. These were so expensive with respect to the profit gained that some haciendas went bankrupt. After the first wells were dug there was a lapse in activity, and political pressure for a large irrigation project to derive water from the Pisco River or the Andean plateau was strong.[25] Well drilling was resumed about 1930 (apparently when efforts to build the irrigation project met with political failure); several wells were dug in Ocucaje at that time. By 1937 there were wells in all parts of the valley; in 1939 their number had increased to forty-nine.[26] Many more wells were dug in the 1940's, when the war-inflated price of cotton made additional capital investment feasible. There are now over 600 wells in the valley (including the Pampa de los Castillos). Extensive pumping has lowered the water table, and the wells in the valley have suffered a consequent decrease in output. More fuel must be burned to pump the same amount of water, making it more expensive than before.

The cost of digging and equipping wells has limited them to the wealthier landowners, and since a good well frees a farmer from dependence on the summer floods, the consequent changes in irrigation practice also began with the wealthier operators. The short duration of the floods often made it necessary to employ check dams or settlement basins; as soon as well irrigation was adopted, furrow irrigation followed on the large properties which had wells. When medium owners, who could not afford to equip a well, began to buy water from the larger operators in the 1940's, they, too, began furrow irrigation of their cotton. The practice of buying well water has recently been extended to small owners, but they have not replaced their *pozas* with open, furrowed fields

[25] Fuchs 1905; Marsters 1908, 1909; Sutton 1905, 1907. The project to bring water from the Andean Plateau was completed in 1959. See page 8.
[26] Conkling 1939.

29

for several reasons. First, they only buy water occasionally and are still heavily dependent on the floods, which must be directed to and held in *pozas* if irrigation is to be effective; second, they usually plant cotton in areas which already contain established vineyards (in *pozas*) which they are loath to abandon.

Pumping irrigation water for sale began as an adjunct to the other agricultural activities of well owners, but it has become a business in its own right. Almost all haciendas sell water to neighboring medium and small farmers when they themselves do not need it, and one entrepreneur has built wells in an area of small-holders with the express purpose of selling water; he does not own any agricultural land. The most important factor of water selling is that the purchase of water obliges the buyer to grow cotton. Many water sellers take their payment only in cotton, and even if they took cash, only cotton would render a sufficient profit to make well irrigation worthwhile.[27]

SUMMARY

All of these associated changes — cotton cultivation, well irrigation, cash payment, mechanization, crop loans — have been filtering down through successive levels of rural society since the 1940's, but they have not yet penetrated fully to the small farmers. It is to be expected, however, that the small farmers will eventually accept all of those innovations which they can afford economically. The adoption of these modern activities is but the last phase of a process of agricultural acculturation that began in the colonial period with the acceptance of grape cultivation by the Indians and their early incorporation into a cash-oriented, market-sensitive economy in which they clearly occupied an exploitable and inferior position.

Many of the recent changes in the agricultural field have been those of increased centralization of capital and of political and economic power. The wageworker is directly dependent on his employer for support and no longer has the security of a small plot of land on which to grow his food. Instead of the traditional guar-

[27] Large owners do irrigate vines with well water, but the wells are the same ones that they use to irrigate their cotton.

antees accorded a sharecropper, he has the government's social security provisions to protect him in time of need. Maximum efficiency in the new cotton-based economy is possible only on a mechanized basis, but the small peasant cannot assemble the necessary capital to mechanize his operations. Thus, he is at a disadvantage when in competition with the large landowners. Some cooperative mechanization has begun, but it is minor in scope; only time will tell whether the small owners will band together in associations to make maximum use of their lands. Most of the efforts of small peasants toward modernization, as in the purchase of well water on credit, place them more firmly under the economic control of large owners. The increased economic control of large owners is also illustrated by the greater concentration of agricultural land in their hands in recent years. On the governmental level, we have seen how control of irrigation has been taken out of the hands of a multitude of local political bosses and placed in the hands of fewer, but more powerful, nationally-oriented politicians.

Some of the aspects of concentration of wealth and economic power are more clearly illustrated in the chapter on industry which follows. Further examples of the centralization of political power will be given in the chapters on social class. It should not be thought, however, that these changes presage the coming of some Orwellian oligarchy in Ica. In fact, they are aspects of its passing, for this increased centralization of power over rural life affects a much smaller proportion of the total population because of the marked urbanization of the valley. While it is perfectly true that the modern social, political, and economic structure of Ica is more stringent in some ways than it was, it is more permissive in others. Further, the new class of skilled laborers necessary to operate the complex machines now in use is not without latent power, and it exercises that power on ever more frequent occasions. The same process that places great wealth in the hands of a few men makes them heavily dependent on a corps of skilled workers who are irreplaceable because of their intricate knowledge and who are essential to the maintenance of the system.

CHAPTER FOUR

Industry

Wine and Liquor. As we saw in the preceding chapter, cultivation of the grapevine was popular in Ica from an early date. The principal early use of the grape was not as a food, but as the source for wine, and sometime in the seventeenth century the distillation of *pisco* (grape brandy) also became important.[1] Before *pisco* was distilled, none of the wine was fortified; afterward the brandy was added either to fresh must or to young wine (*cachina*) to make a fortified sweet wine (*vino generoso*).

While cultivation of the grape extended rapidly throughout the society, from wealthy Spaniards to tributary Indians, wine-making did not. Indians sold their grapes to the Spaniards or possibly trod them and sold the must,[2] but the Spaniards made the wine.[3] The

[1] Sánchez Elías 1957:43.
[2] J. H. Rowe, personal communication.
[3] Anonymous MS.

retarded diffusion of wine-making to the poorer segments of the population is largely explainable on economic grounds. Wine-making is a process requiring extensive facilities; it is expensive, risky, and usually yields a delayed profit. The tributary Indians were in no position to make the capital investment necessary to produce wine.

Some of the wine was consumed in the valley, and the Indians reportedly distinguished themselves in this, even if they played a small part in its production.[4] About 1600 most of the wine was shipped by donkey train to the small port of Morro Quemado on the Bahía de la Independencia; smaller amounts were sent to Pisco for embarkation or to the sierra. Part of the eventual market for Iquenian wine was within Peru, while some wine was destined for Mexico, Guatemala, or even the Philippines, despite a variety of royal decrees prohibiting its shipment and even the cultivation of the grape.[5]

Because of the variable capacity of wine jars and the fact that statements of quantity were usually made in terms of jars rather than a more specific liquid measure, it is difficult to arrive at an accurate estimate of the amount of wine produced. The difficulty is compounded by the fact that fortified wines contained a varying amount of *pisco*, which was in turn distilled from young wine. Nevertheless, the valley probably produced 500 times as much wine in 1639 as in 1574.[6] The rapid growth and great amount of wine production indicate its importance to the valley. Further indications are offered by the fact that wine served as a medium of exchange, even for the purchase of slaves.[7]

Other Industries. Large potteries for wine jars (*botijas*), glass

[4] Cobo 1956:392.

[5] See Picasso 1944.

[6] I have attempted to reduce colonial data to metric statements of the basic amounts of must produced, in liters, for the following years:

1574	24,000	(Sánchez Elías 1957:41)
1590	1,800,000	(Morúa 1946:194–195)
1605	6,000,000	(Anonymous MS)
1617	5,000,000	(Vásquez de Espinosa 1948:449)
1639 { min.	8,000,000	
1639 { max.	11,000,000	(Calancha 1639:755)

[7] Sánchez Elías 1957:40–42.

factories, mines, and smelters also functioned in the valley during colonial times, and many smaller industries were known. The archaeologically known pottery is abundant and of good quality. Other minor goods, such as carts, furniture, tools, and clothing, were made as well.[8]

THE REPUBLICAN AND EARLY MODERN PERIOD (1820–1910)

Wine and Liquor. The manufacture of wine and *pisco* continued to be the principal industry of the valley until about the end of the nineteenth century. Brandy, however, became increasingly important within the industry, and several technical changes in processing are probably associated with the emphasis on distillation. The beam press, for example, probably came into use during the republican period, but its exact antiquity in Ica is uncertain.[9] When it was utilized in extruding the must, the marc was soaked and pressed in order to extract the more flavorful and astringent materials from the grapes. Wines made in this fashion are usually of inferior quality, but the process is particularly useful in brandy-making in order to give more flavor to the spirits. Rather late in the republican period, certainly not before 1860, the emphasis on brandy production led to the adoption of more efficient, coiled exhaust tubes in the stills at larger distilleries. These were known as *serpentines* or *alambiques*, in contrast to the earlier *falcas* (pot-stills with straight exhaust tubes).

The de-emphasis of naturally fermented wines produced from local grapes implied in the changes described above was supported by another development in the industry. Beginning about 1840 on

[8] Only the principal industries will be treated in detail here; for information on potteries, glass factories, mining, and handicrafts see Hammel 1959.

[9] The type of ancient beam press which is found in Ica is common on the Iberian peninsula and used for pressing marc (Dias 1948:34, 96–97, 119 ff.; 1953:121) and olives (G. M. Foster, personal communication); it is known from Italy as well (Forbes 1955:133 ff.). It has been in use at least since 25 B.C. without major changes in design, and the details of its use do not seem to have changed since Roman times (Drachmann 1932:147, fig. 15; Forbes 1955:133 ff.). Thus, it could have been brought to Ica as early as viticulture itself. However, none of the early travellers mention the beam press, and informants in Ica usually gave a maximum age of "about 100 years" for those still in existence.

34

the estates of Domingo Elías [10] and later at the wineries of wealthy Italian immigrants, many trials were made with newly introduced varieties of grapes to produce European-type table and fortified wines. The comments of nineteenth-century travelers such as Tschudi indicate that the local wine was distastefully heavy to the non-Iberian palate, being derived from an inferior grape. The wine industry existed primarily for export, and both the change to European-type wines and the emphasis on the more acceptable *pisco* were based on an effort to maintain the export volume which the valley had enjoyed in colonial times.[11]

By 1875, not only large owners were making wine and distilling brandy; the practice had been adopted by owners of medium-sized plots as well. Usually only those farmers holding at least ten hectares of land had stills. Most of the smaller still owners had only *falcas*, rather than *alambiques*, and pressed the marc by piling rocks on it instead of using an elaborate press. The number of functioning stills in the valley in 1900 was about 250.[12]

Production of the wine and *pisco* probably reached its high point during this period.[13]

Cotton Ginning. The commercial production of cotton was begun in Ica by Ismael Elías, a wealthy planter, in 1844,[14] and in all probability he had his own cotton gin. Cotton production in 1846 was only 150 metric tons (M.T.), but it had increased twelvefold by 1887.[15] This increase indicates that the rise of the cotton industry in Ica, as elsewhere in Peru, was fostered by the collapse of the industry in the United States following the Civil War. Pro-

[10] Tschudi 1847:234–235.
[11] See also Chabert and Dubosc 1908.
[12] Based on fragmentary data from the Caja de Depósitos y Consignaciones, Ica.
[13] The basic amounts of must, in liters, produced in three sample years were:

1846	25,000,000 (Castelnau 1851:164)
1855	20,000,000 (González Herrera n.d.:205)
1903	7,500,000 (Sutton 1905, 1907; Chabert and Dubosc 1908)

The decline in yield by 1903 was in part caused by the great age of the vines, in part by exhaustion of the soil, and by other factors. See the section on the modern period.
[14] *Peru Today* 1912.
[15] Castelnau 1851:164; González Herrera n.d.:205.

duction declined to 1100 M.T. in 1903,[16] possibly as a result of the recuperation of the American South.

Most early gins were on haciendas. There was one in Ocucaje in 1862,[17] and by 1888 there were at least five, all in rural areas.[18] In 1904, there were about two gins in the city of Ica, two in the rural areas of the valley, and seven more scattered through the Palpa and Nasca valleys. Thus, the dispersed character of the industry was still evident at the turn of the century. Even in 1912, when there were three gins in the city, there was at least one in the rural part of the valley and ten more in Palpa and Nasca. Dispersal of industry continued to be characteristic of outlying, more provincial areas until the cotton boom of World War I and subsequent developments in motorized transportation. Since centralization of industry reached its peak in the modern period, discussion of the factors involved will be deferred to the following section.

Other Industries. The manufacture of wine jars continued at least until the turn of the century, but nowhere in the literature is there any mention of the old glass factories.[19] A textile factory with eighty to eighty-five looms for the manufacture of coarse cloth was established in the city in 1903; its products were sold locally and shipped to Bolivia.[20] Copper was mined intermittently in the Canzas area (La Tinguiña) until 1873, and mining activity increased after that date under the partnership of Narducci and Meiggs. Mining ceased after 1884 because the ores were practically exhausted and the predominantly Chilean miners had returned to their own country during the war between Peru and Chile. Higher taxes on copper and increased shipping costs on the Ica–Pisco railroad inhibited any recovery of the industry, although there was some minor scavenging activity between 1899 and 1902, prompted by a brief rise in the price of copper. [21]

[16] Sutton 1905, 1907.
[17] Raimondi 1945:9.
[18] González Herrera n.d.:205.
[19] Raimondi 1945 contains a good description of the manufacture of wine jars in 1862.
[20] Garland n.d.:115; Marie 1916:89.
[21] Fuchs 1905:10–12.

Wine and Liquor. The wineries and distilleries of Ica were in a difficult economic position at the turn of the century. The traditional sweet, natural wines and the heavy fortified wines of the valley were no longer as acceptable for export as they had been in the colonial period, and attempts were being made to produce lighter wines of the French and Italian types. At the same time, the great age of many vines, poor care, sporadic droughts, and lack of fertilization had caused the yield of must to drop from an earlier figure of 62–75 hectoliters per hectare to only 25.[22] Even the fiery and popular *pisco* was losing ground to the common *aguardiente* (*cañazo*) made on the northern coast, and there were frequent attempts to adulterate *pisco* with cane sugar in Ica.

The already precarious situation of the wine industry was prejudiced further by the initial rise of the competing cotton industry. Large owners began to replace vineyards with cotton fields around 1905, and the practice has since extended to medium landowners. The majority of the old wineries and distilleries have been abandoned; there are only 100 functioning stills in Ica now, and three-quarters of these produce only a small amount of *pisco* or wine.

Most of the data point to an irreversible decline in the wine industry, and, indeed, most of the inhabitants of Ica regard the industry as one destined to disappear. Nevertheless, the average annual production of must from 1945 to 1956 was ten million liters, a third more than that produced about 1900. Even more significant is the fact that the ten million liters were produced on half the acreage devoted to vineyards in 1900. Thus, the efficiency of wine production has more than doubled in the last half-century because of certain economic and technical factors.

All the light table wines and most of the sweet wines and brandy are now produced by four or five major wineries which are all owned by planters who also cultivate large cotton fields. The heavy capital investment necessary to maintain a winery or distillery, to change its processes (by producing new types of wines

[22] Chabert and Dubosc 1908; Marie 1916:80 ff.; *Peru Today* 1911; Romero 1939; Sutton 1905, 1907.

or installing modern machinery), and to make the light European wines, which require some maturation, have been supported by the profits from cotton cultivation. The large wineries have also been able to fertilize their vineyards, cultivate in a more modern way, and give occasional, more beneficial, light irrigations with the water from wells which they usually use to irrigate their cotton. Spoilage and evaporation in the wineries have been diminished by the installation of modern concrete fermenting tanks, pumping systems, and imported European-style casks. The major portion of the wine industry is more intensive than ever before, even if it has suffered a decrease in area cultivated (since 1900) and a decrease in total production (compared to the high point about 1846). An interesting ethnic sidelight on the changes in the industry is that Italians made most of the innovations (ca. 1860 and later), and they now own or staff most of the large wineries.

Traditional wine-making and distilling continue, although on a reduced scale. Not only are there fewer traditional establishments in operation but any one of these produces less wine and *pisco* than it did before. There has been some modernization of equipment in a few traditional wineries; some of these use a direct-screw press of iron (like a North American cider press) instead of the unwieldy beam press, but most function just as they did a century ago.[23] Some medium landowners still use old *falcas* to make *pisco* for home consumption.

Cotton Ginning and Oil Extraction. By 1911 the amount of cotton ginned in the valley had recovered from its low point of 1903 and regained the level enjoyed in 1887. By 1915 the valley experienced an increase of another third, and by 1929 production stood at almost four times the 1911 level. Much of this increase resulted from the high wartime price of cotton and the generally inflated world market after the armistice. The depression dropped production to the 1915 level, and not until another war, in 1939, stimulated the market did production reach its 1929 height. In-

[23] The design of the direct-screw press is also old in Western culture and was known to Pliny (Forbes 1955). See Blanchard 1929: fig. 9, for an example of current use of the press in Iberia.

creased demand since that time has raised current annual production to over ten times the amount ginned in 1887 or 1911.[24]

The pre-World War I rise in production was accompanied by an increase in the number of cotton gins. There was at least one oil mill for extracting cotton seed oil by 1916 [25] and there were ten gins in the valley in 1929, six of them in the city. At least two of the urban gins had oil mills; that is a more significant increase over the 1916 figure than it would appear, since the increasing cultivation of Tangüis and Egipto (American Upland) cotton made oil extraction a more complicated process.[26]

Despite the rapid increase in cotton production since the early 1930's, the number of cotton gins has *decreased*. There are seven in the valley, two of which are in the rural area. Actually, only one of the rural gins is successful, and it remains a profitable enterprise solely because it is located on a very large hacienda, whose owners control over 3,000 hectares of cotton-producing land in the valley. The two largest urban gins include modern oil mills and are owned by foreign interests; they process most of the cotton and all the seed from the Ica-Nasca-Palpa area.[27] This greater specialization and concentration of the ginning and oil-milling industry have been made possible by the increased use of motor transport in recent years. Except under unusual circumstances, such as those cited above, it is not profitable for a hacienda to maintain a private gin. The increased capacity and the higher economic status of the two major urban gin enterprises have also been due in large

[24] Estimates of cotton production in the valley are as follows:

Year	Cotton (metric tons)	Year	Cotton (metric tons)
1903	1100	1931	2600
1911	1820	1939	6500
1915	2400	1956	19,000
1929	6500		

[25] Marie 1916.

[26] Egipto and Tangüis seed must be cleaned in a special second gin, a "linter," before crushing. The seed of the native El País cotton is not hairy and can be processed directly after the first ginning. See Marie 1916.

[27] Seed production in the Province of Ica in 1962 was 8.65 million quintals (1 quintal = 220.46 pounds), 166 percent of production in 1953. (Perú, Cámara Algodonera, Memoria anual 1962, Anexos 13, 14).

part to their role as bankers. They finance most of the cotton growing in the valley by making cash advances on expected crops, and much of their effort is directed toward encouraging and supervising this crop. They give technical advice to their clients, and one enterprise owns a large plantation which also functions as a cotton experimental station.

Other Industries. No trace of the wine-jar industry remains, although old men can recall having seen the jars made when they were boys. The major wineries, as noted, now use concrete fermenting vats, and the smaller establishments are too few and produce too little to support *botija* potteries. The old firing ovens have fallen into decay, although a few are still employed to make bricks. Even in brick-making (as in other minor industries) there has been a notable specialization and concentration of effort. Medium owners used to make their own bricks, as did the haciendas, but now, most bricks are produced in large quantities by a few specialists.

Some copper mining is carried on in the Canzas area and in the upper valley near Huamaní, but it contributes practically nothing to the economy of the valley. The textile factory has passed into the hands of a wealthy Italian entrepreneur but is much less important than it used to be, employing about twenty-five persons and producing only coarse yarn for bags. All the finer cloth comes from Lima instead of being produced locally.

SUMMARY

Ica's industry has always been dependent on the export market and has been part of the European economic sphere for four hundred years. Its dependence on the world market may be illustrated by the changes in the wine industry, which were made to please overseas palates, and by the immediate reactions (in fluctuating production levels) to wartime and depression price changes in cotton. Awareness in Ica of the importance of world economic conditions extends even to small farmers; I can recall the apprehension they showed in 1958 when the U.S. Secretary of Agriculture threw large quantities of surplus cotton on the world market.

An increasing specialization of effort is also discernible in Ica's industrial history. The valley was largely self-sufficient in the colonial period, particularly with respect to the consumption patterns of the lower class, but today, even the needs of the poorest highlander are supplied from Lima rather than from the valley itself. The importation of cloth instead of its local production is an example of the change. In those industries which continue to operate, specialization is no less evident: The wineries and cotton gins have become highly technical and intensively operated factories. Their numbers have decreased, but their efficiency and the consequent levels of production have increased. Even the brick kilns have followed the same pattern.

Another kind of change can be seen in the financial aspects of industrial development. The earlier establishments (wineries, gins) were operated by local landowners. Now they are owned by entrepreneurs who have other business interests in the valley, in Peru, or in other countries. Many of these businessmen are Italians, and as an ethnic group they have undisputed economic control of the valley.

While the principal "causes" of these trends lie in the steadily increasing connection with European and North American markets and in the increased concentration of capital necessary to support major industrial enterprise, the changes are also bound up closely with parallel developments in transportation. Since the profit-making incentive and an increasing need to export were part of the general climate of industrial development in Ica, a feature of that development was a progressive maximization of efficiency in the rapid movement of large amounts of goods.

The developments outlined above have been concerned largely with the ownership and operation of industry. The other side of the coin — developments in the labor force — is equally interesting, although historical documentation for it is poorer. Specialization of labor has been just as characteristic of the developmental process as centralization of ownership. Any husky peasant can tread grapes, walk behind a plow, or open an irrigation gate, but not every man can operate a mechanical grapeshredder, level a field using modern equipment, or adjust the injectors on a diesel pumping engine. The availability of a skilled labor pool is as necessary to the establishment and maintenance of industry as abundant capital.

Most of the skilled laborers in Ica have come from peasant families within the last generation. They no longer have the security of a peasant subsistence economy to support them, but their economic position is buttressed occasionally by the protections of organized labor and generally by the regulations of a paternalistic government which has taken over many functions of the old *patrón*. The integral role of the laboring class in Ica society has more aspects than the economic one outlined here, but they are deferred to later chapters. For example, a strike of bank clerks can paralyze the national economy for two months, and such strikes and other mass demonstrations have been effective in changing the policies of the national government in recent years. Unlike the slaves and tributaries of the colonial period whose sole recourse was to rise in armed revolt only to be smashed by superior forces (which even happened to the Iquenian peasants at Parcona earlier in this century), the lower classes can now withhold their services long enough to exercise power without destroying their economic position.

CHAPTER FIVE

Transportation
and Trade

Before the Spanish conquest, most traveling in the valley was on
foot. Burdens were usually carried for short distances by men, and
important persons may also have been transported in litters by
human bearers; the llama was certainly used as a pack animal in
prehistoric times.[1]

Specific evidence of trade between Ica and other areas is scarce
because of the high degree of artistic similarity between the pottery styles of the valley and neighboring areas in most periods,
particularly before A.D. 1000. After that time the styles of the
coast diverged sufficiently so that some inferences on inter-valley
trade are possible. Ica-like vessels have been found in the Nasca

---

[1] Designs of llamas with halters are found on some pottery vessels of the
Nasca 2 style, ca. A.D. 250, and extensive deposits of llama bones are known
from the period A.D. 1300–1500.

43

drainage, and some more typical of the Nasca drainage have been discovered in Ica for the period about 1300.[2] Some Chincha-like pottery has been found in Ica dating around 1400, as well as vessels of the highland Inca type which may antedate Inca occupation of the valley.[3] The pottery styles of the Pisco Valley after 1300 show strong influence from Ica; historical and modern sources tell of Iquenian Indians going to the Pisco Valley to plant food crops during exceptionally severe droughts in their own valley. Thus, while the evidence is not highly specific or conclusive, it does indicate trade and culture contact of limited range existed between Ica and nearby areas.

THE COLONIAL AND EARLY REPUBLICAN PERIOD (1533–1875)

The beasts of burden and vehicles introduced by the Spaniards had a notable effect on local transportation: Horses were used by members of the upper class for riding and drawing their carriages. The donkey became the most popular beast of burden, transporting goods and carrying members of the lower class, but it was not used to draw vehicles or plows except under unusual circumstances. Oxen were employed chiefly in plowing but also served to draw high, two-wheeled carts with stake sides. Mules are rarely mentioned in the historical sources, although they were occasionally used for riding, and some were trained in the same gaits as the horses. The use of mules for plowing did not commence until about 1900.

Most commercial shipping was done by donkey train. Wines were transported from Ica to Morro Quemado, the southern cape of the Bahía de la Independencia, for transportation by boat to Lima, Arica, and other points. Some wine was also sent to Pisco for embarkation.[4] The route to Morro Quemado led over the barren Tablazo de Ica, either from Ocucaje or from the city of Ica (via Comatrana or the lake of La Huega). The Pisco road led from the city through San Juan Bautista, El Carmen and the site of modern Guadalupe, across the lower Pampa de Chunchanga to

2 Hammel, Norsworthy, and Rowe MS; Menzel MS.
3 Menzel MS.
4 Vásquez de Espinosa 1948:449.

the Hacienda Villacurí, where there was an overnight stop. The rest of the road lay over the Pisco Pampa to the port. Another road to Pisco led from Huamaní over the intervening ridges to Humay in the middle Pisco Valley, then downriver to the sea.

There was also some trade with the sierra mostly carried by llama train. Ica lay on one of the roads from Lima to Cuzco, via Nasca, Puquio, and Abancay, and many travellers passed through the valley. The volume of traffic was sufficient in the early colonial period to support two roadside inns (*ventas*). Local trade between Ica and the neighboring sierra was heaviest along the road to Córdova, up the Tingue Valley, and there was some trade with settlements in the Yauca Valley. Less travel took place through the main canyon of the Ica because of the more precipitous terrain between Huamaní and Santiago de Chocorvos. Nevertheless, there were routes from Ica to the latter and to Castrovirreyna.

THE LATE REPUBLICAN AND EARLY MODERN PERIOD (1875–1910)

Commercial traffic out of the valley began to funnel more and more toward Pisco, and the port at Morro Quemado fell into disuse. The volume of traffic was great enough by the 1870's to warrant building the Pisco–Ica railroad, and the track was completed in 1875. The principal effect of the railhead in Ica was to channel great quantities of goods through the city for shipment, while the old donkey tracks leading from rural areas out of the valley to the north and west were no longer used. The cart traffic to Ica from Los Molinos alone amounted to 2000 tons per year about 1910. Efforts were made to construct a railroad from Los Molinos to Ica and to extend the Pisco–Ica line to Lima, but they were never realized.[5]

Travel was a lengthy and often dangerous affair at the turn of the century. A trip from Los Molinos to Ica required three hours, from Huamaní, five. Pisco was two days away from Ica by foot or horse, and a day by train. Lima was a week's journey by land; most travellers went to Pisco and continued to Lima by ship. The pack trains from the Bahía de la Independencia which brought fish to the valley spent fourteen hours on the desert road, although a

[5] Fuchs 1905; González Herrera n.d.: 214; *Peru Today* 1912.

man without animals could make the distance in nine hours by running down the slopes of the hills to gain time. Journeys were dangerous because of the many bandits in the thick huarango forests who preyed on travellers.

Despite the concentration of shipping activity in the city because of the railhead, the general pattern of trade was the same as it had been a century earlier. Ica was connected to the outside world through Pisco, and almost all its exports left via that port. Some trade was carried on with the neighboring sierra, and from this period come the first reports of the bartering of cheese and potatoes for wine and *pisco* between the highlanders and the peasants of the valley, but the practice was probably an old one. Occasional llama trains laden with highland produce still came down the Tingue Valley from Córdova. Within the Ica Valley, local transportation continued to follow the old donkey roads.

THE LATE MODERN PERIOD (1910–1957)

Motorized transport made its first impression on Ica between 1910 and 1920 in the form of a one-cylinder Reo car which had come overland from Pisco because the railroad refused to carry such a dangerous machine! A little later, a motor bike was introduced; it made a triumphant circuit around the main plaza and then exploded. The number of vehicles was small at first, but increased at a gradually accelerating rate. In 1921 there were probably 30 trucks and 85 automobiles in the Province of Ica (valleys of Ica and Palpa).[6] By 1956 the Province of Ica had over 1500 trucks, 300 private cars, 500 taxis, and 200 omnibusses. The growth of motorized transport has been unequal among the several types of vehicles, illustrating the purposes of the vehicles and the economic resources necessary to acquire them. The highest rate of increase has been in trucks, which are used for commercial and agricultural purposes by wealthy owners. Private cars and busses have increased somewhat less; the cars are the transportation of the wealthy and the busses of the rest of the population. The smallest increase has

[6] No early data for the Province of Ica (Ica-Palpa) are available, but subsequent figures indicate that the Ica-Palpa area usually contained about half the vehicles in the overall Ica-Nasca zone, which had 59 trucks and 171 automobiles in 1921.

been in taxis, which are owned by middle-class operators but used by persons somewhat above them in the social scale. Mechanization has been a real process, moreover, not just an apparent one, since the number of vehicles has increased faster than the population or agricultural production. Relative to the loads they carry, private cars have increased most rapidly, with busses, trucks, and taxis following in that order. It is important to note that private cars, which are definite symbols of prestige as well as utilitarian objects, have had the greatest rate of increase.[7]

Routes of communication changed markedly as a result of the increased use of motorized transport. Generally speaking, more goods travel over fewer roads than before. While travel for short distances among the lower classes is still by foot or donkey, as in going to the fields or delivering produce to village homes, most trips of over five kilometers are taken by vehicle. Because the country roads are bumpy and narrow, most vehicles use the Pan-American Highway as much as possible.[8]

In the 1930's automobiles were making the trip to Lima over the unpaved highway in two days. Travel was still dangerous because of the bandits, the last of whom were shot into their graves about 1935 by the father of the present alcalde of Ica. It is said that drivers on the Ica–Lima run in the 1930's used to carry loaded pistols on the seats beside them and sometimes had to shoot their way through ambushes and roadblocks. Agricultural produce from the sides of the valley was brought to the main highway on donkey or llama back to be reloaded onto trucks as late as the 1930's, and some llama trains were still coming into the city from Córdova at that time. Most goods were still shipped from Ica to Pisco by rail, but the paving of the Pan-American Highway in the 1930's cut sharply into the carriage of the railroad. The ratio of railroad tonnage to trucks in 1934 was 211:1 but had dropped to 8:1 by

[7] The absolute number of trucks in 1956 had increased by a factor of 17 since 1924, private cars by 12, taxis by 7, and busses by 10. With respect to relative increases, in 1924 there were 1250 persons per private car or taxi, 3900 per bus, and 132 metric tons of produce per truck. In 1956 there were 150 persons per private auto, 260 per taxi, 520 per bus, and 18 metric tons of produce per truck. Thus, relative to their loads, private cars increased nine times, taxis five, busses eight, and trucks seven.

[8] See Pitt-Rivers 1954 for a similar situation in rural Spain.

1953. For several years, the railroad subsisted almost entirely on the business given it by one large cotton gin and oil mill; the last engine exploded in 1955 and was never replaced. The tracks have now been removed.

Paving of the highway and demise of the railroad had the further effect that many goods were shipped directly to Lima instead of to Pisco for embarkation. The ratio of tonnage exported from Pisco to the agricultural production of the valley was five times greater in 1933 than in 1951. The decline of the port of Pisco, relative to the productivity of its hinterland, is properly material for another study, but it is interesting that many Peruvian ports have suffered the same decline over the years. In the colonial period each valley had its own port, and many haciendas had private facilities for shipping. Now, even the major provincial ports such as Pisco have suffered a decrease in tonnage, and most shipping activity is concentrated in the single port of Callao (the port of Lima).[9]

The modern pattern of transportation and trade is thus vastly different from what it was. Huamaní is less than two hours from the city, and cars travel to Pisco in only an hour on the modern highway. Lima is only three or four hours by car, of more convenient access to the city of Ica than many points within the valley. The truck tonnage exported from Ica in 1956 amounted to over 60,000 metric tons, and the amount passing through the valley is much higher because of its position on the main north-south highway of the country. The facility of auto travel to other coastal points has even inhibited the development of an airfield in Ica.[10]

SUMMARY

The social aspects of these changes have been manifold. Instead of cartwrights, harness-makers, and muleteers, Ica has automobile

[9] Despite the decline in activity resulting from diversion of much shipping to Callao, Pisco remained the foremost export point for cotton during 1953–1962. Perú, Cámara Algodonera, Memoria anual 1962, Anexo 30.

[10] There was some commercial air traffic between Ica and Lima in the 1930's, but the paving of the highway and consequent ease of auto travel have resulted in its abandonment.

mechanics and truck drivers. Besides straightforward occupational changes, there have been those of the expanded horizons of the population. Before the railroad was built, the brides of provincial gentlemen, if they came from Lima to Ica, never expected to see the capital again until after their children were grown. Even the busy muleteers knew little of the country beyond Nasca or Pisco. Now it is quite different. Persons of the upper class visit Lima almost every weekend and even drive there for a dinner engagement, returning to Ica the next day. Peasant women who had not left their native district all their lives shop daily in Ica and make occasional trips to Pisco or Lima to visit relatives.

This expansion, however, has been only along the Pan-American Highway and principally in the direction of Lima. While upper-class individuals look upon weekends in Lima as a necessary part of their existence, only the more intrepid of them have driven south to Arequipa. Very few have ever been to the sierra, other than to take a quick airplane flight from Lima to Cuzco. The peasants and lower urban classes follow the same pattern; if they travel any great distance, it is to Lima. Very few rural dwellers from the San Juan area have ever been to the southern part of the valley around Santiago; almost none of them have been to isolated spots such as Ocucaje and Huamaní. None of them have ever gone to the neighboring sierra.[11]

The channelling of traffic along the Pan-American Highway and the funnelling of local traffic from rural areas first into the city of Ica for exit from the valley, have had effects on more than just commercial relations. They have, for example, influenced the marriage patterns of rural areas. The frequency of selection of a spouse from outside one's village or district is greater now than it was a generation ago, and the distance from which spouses are obtained has increased. However, there is a tendency to select a spouse either from one's own half of the valley, *or* from outside the val-

[11] This narrow orientation is changing. In the last few years upper-class individuals in Ica, as elsewhere in Peru, have been embarking upon their own "age of discovery" and are finding out that there is more to their country than 300 kilometers of coastal highway. The lower classes do not seem to have participated in the change yet, except in unusual cases.

ley, but not from the other half of the valley, a pattern paralleling the division of the valley into two halves by the focal point of Ica City in the communications network.[12]

[12] In rural San Juan Bautista District, marriages in 1956 were still 80 percent village-endogamous with respect to place of immediate premarital residence and 65 percent village-endogamous with respect to place of birth, but the degree of endogamy is less than it was a generation ago. At the district level, the endogamy rate with respect to place of birth was 68 percent, as opposed to 79 percent a generation ago. Of the district-exogamous marriages, 66 percent were contracted within the North Valley in the present generation, while about 80 percent of them were contracted in that compass in the last generation. Thus, the degree of endogamy has decreased, *and* exogamous marriages are now more frequently made beyond the confines of the rural district. Marriages which are made beyond the confines of the district, however, are still concentrated in the North Valley (66 percent); only 2 percent were contracted with persons from the South Valley, while 29 percent were contracted with persons from other coastal locations. Even marriages with the culturally different highlanders occur in greater frequency than those with persons from the South Valley. For further details see Hammel 1964c.

CHAPTER SIX

The
History of
Power in Ica

"Power" is used here in its most general and all-inclusive Weberian sense: economic control, political authority, and prestige are all varieties of power. The manipulation of wealth or even the withholding of labor can force the acquiescence of others, the legal right to command and the threat or use of force are kinds of power, and even prestige and social honor which require deference constitute power. That power is a complex sum of attributes and advantages, and that any society, however minimally hierarchical, has more than one dimension have been recognized by almost all theorists and analysts of human affairs.[1] In fact, the nature of power and of its distribution is so complex that mere description

---

[1] The original suggestion of a tridimensional structuring seems to have been made by Weber (1958). See also Nadel 1951 for a two-dimensional suggestion, and the reformulation to three dimensions in Hammel 1959, 1962a. A recent major theoretical work on the problem is Lenski 1966.

poses grave problems of communication. Historical treatment is even more difficult, sharing the problems involved, let us say, in the simultaneous description of the harmony and the melodic line of a complex symphony. This chapter will summarize the economic history that has gone before, primarily in terms of the hierarchical locus of control of wealth, and will add to these materials a commentary on the history of political authority. Consideration of status honor will be deferred largely to the following chapter.

The society of Ica is not a homogeneous one, overall or in any of its segments, and it has had a marked hierarchical structure for at least 500 years. Wealth, power, and prestige have been intertwined in complex ways, with one dimension seemingly ascendant at one time, with mobility possible in one dimension but not in another at a different time, with the congruence of the three dimensions shifting from one rigidity to another. Even the rigidity has been subject to change. Mobility has always been possible in Ica, but it has been more possible at some times than at others, more along one dimension than along a second. The language of social position has also changed, so that the symbols in terms of which members of the society communicated their understandings and mutual expectations about social position and the distribution of social resources went through their own evolution.[2] It is with all these kinds of change that we are concerned.[3]

THE PRECONQUEST PERIOD (TO 1533)

We know nothing of the pre-Inca social organization of the valley in a direct sense, although we can speculate from the evidence of archaeological remains that major wealth differences did exist in the population. Even in the Inca period we have no direct knowledge of what the valley was like but must reason by analogy with

[2] See Hammel 1964b.

[3] For details on stratum culture in Ica and on urban-rural differences, see Hammel 1959, 1961, 1962a, 1962b, 1964a. For pertinent comparative materials and theoretical discussion see Álvarez Andrews 1951; Beals 1953; Crevenna 1951; Davidson 1947; Foster 1953b; Gillin 1947b; Goldkind 1965, 1966; Goldschmidt 1950; Hawthorn 1948; Patch 1966; Wagley and Harris 1955; Whiteford 1960; Whitten 1965; Wolf 1955, 1956.

other portions of the Inca Empire for which there is better documentary evidence. In briefest outline, the society of Ica must have been arranged under the Inca Empire as follows.[4]

The society was essentially a two-class system of nobles and commoners. Among the nobles, the Inca class was superior and controlled the Empire as a whole, ruling from the heartland of Cuzco and occasionally having representatives among the ruling classes of the provinces. The lesser nobility was composed of local rulers who had been subjugated by the Incas and left as administrators of their peoples under the Empire. There were probably no members of the Inca class in Ica, and all political power lay in the hands of the local nobles. The great mass of commoners was composed largely of taxpayers (able-bodied adult males) and their families, together with a number of hereditary or appointed servants and officials. All nobles were exempt from payment of taxes and forced labor service, but they were responsible for overseeing and arranging the fulfillment of the taxpayers' obligations. The taxpayers paid their tribute to the Empire in the form of group labor on the fields of the Inca and the state church and were, in addition, subject to rotating individual service in the postal network and other branches of the government. The hereditary servants paid no taxes of this kind but worked exclusively for the state and were supported by it. The Inca system of regulating land tenure among the commoners probably led to a minimum of wealth differences in the lower class. On the other hand, the gradations of status among the nobles were extremely complicated, and each rung of the prestige ladder was marked by special symbols in dress and the degree of ostentation permitted.

The structure of power was monolithic, and the three dimensions of society were closely coordinate. There was some mobility, but it was primarily along the political dimension, and social conflict seems to have centered in this, rather than in the dimensions of wealth or prestige.

[4] Information on the preconquest and colonial periods is based largely on Rowe 1946 and 1957. I am further indebted to Dr. Rowe for some of the unpublished results of his research on the Indians of colonial Ica. See also Gerol 1961; Montell 1929; Moore 1958; Nachtigall 1964.

The Spanish conquest of Peru was a *coup d'état* in which the new rulers took nominal political command of the area from one of the factions in the Peruvian civil war, eliminating the other. Their control of the area did not begin to be effective until about 1565, and the span between their arrival and that date was an extended period of conquest.

The flimsy character of Spanish political control was especially evident in outlying regions such as Ica. For over thirty years after the arrival of the Spaniards the local nobles (*caciques*) continued to rule their own people. They considered that the Spaniards had replaced the Incas and that they owed the Spaniards the same kind of loyalty and tribute that they had granted their former rulers. As a result, they complied with the requests of the *encomenderos* for tribute and labor and probably with the requests of other Spaniards who were not legally entitled to these services under colonial law. The *caciques* were wealthy and influential men in the valley; they entered into business contracts with the Spaniards and held a social status not very much lower than that of the *encomenderos* themselves.[5]

The remainder of the population was composed of the Indian commoners and Negro slaves. There were no direct lines of authority between the last two groups, although non-tributary Indians (*yanaconas*) may have been in charge of slave gangs. The Indians were superior to the slaves in some other ways. They held property, which the slaves did not, but they were subject to tribute, while the slaves were exempt. Generally, the class system of the society was triangular. The Spaniards were in nominal control at the top, the *caciques* just below them and between the Spaniards and the rest of the Indians, and the Indian commoners and slaves on a roughly equal but unrelated footing at the bottom. Spanish political control over the *caciques* was direct, but tenuous; similarly, their superior prestige was formally obvious but obscured by the traditional status of the local nobles. Although the *caciques* did not have direct authority over Negro slaves, some Indians

[5] Cf. Lewis 1960:18.

probably did, even if only as agents of the Spaniards. Although an oppressed class, the tributary Indians were in a superior position to the Negro slaves, although it was an *unrelated* position; their oppression was at least traditional, and they were at the bottom of a separate branch of the structure. The Negro slaves, although theoretically directly under the control of the Spaniards, without intervening *caciques*, were non-persons.

There were, of course, differences of wealth and authority among the Spaniards. The *caciques*, too, were unequal in these respects, and one of the recurrent features of this and the later colonial period was their constant jockeying for position and favor in the eyes of their own subjects and the Spaniards. The Indian commoners, ruled by their own *caciques*, may have had some relatively influential men among them, but it is more likely that most of the positions in the native political structure were held by members of noble families. It is also possible that there were positions of authority among the Negroes, but we have no knowledge of them, and they were not legally recognized under colonial law as were the positions of authority among the Indians.

Realizing that their political position was dangerously weak, the Spaniards set out to tighten their control over Indians *and* Spaniards in the colony. The first city of Ica (the Villa de Valverde) was founded in 1563; one of the stated reasons for its establishment was control of the Spanish population, so that the abuses they were perpetrating against the Indians might be halted. The *reducciones*, or native villages, were established about the same time, and the Indians were grouped together in two villages, Hanan and Lurin, so that they could be more easily controlled and indoctrinated in the Catholic faith. (The first missionary priests did not come to Ica until 1560.) Instead of being administratively responsible to the government in Lima, the *caciques* found themselves under the jurisdiction of a local magistrate (*corregidor*) who also had powers over the local Spaniards. The influence of the *caciques* was materially weakened by the change in organization, as was that of the *encomenderos*. During the next two hundred years the wealth and power of the *caciques* gradually declined, although they retained some of their honorary privileges such as exemption from tribute and personal labor service. At the same time, the process of racial and cultural mixture had been advancing rapidly, so that the scheme of social classes toward the end of the colonial period was something like the following:

The Spaniards were in complete economic and political control of the valley. There were certain differences among them; for example, Spaniards of peninsular birth had greater privileges than those born in the colony (*criollos*, creoles). This distinction between "pure" Spaniards and creoles was one of the weak points in the colonial political structure and was instrumental in the creole revolution of the 1820's. Below the Spaniards in the scale were the *mestizos* (Indian-Spanish mixed bloods); their privileges were considerably fewer than those of persons of pure Caucasian descent. The noble Indians held a legal and social position about equal to that of the *mestizos*, better in some ways and worse in others. Below these classes was the remainder of the population, graded down through an elaborate series of ethno-racial distinctions, each of which had a definite legal status in the colonial system. Unlike the bifurcate or triangular class system of the early colonial period, that of the late colonial period was essentially linear, and the only sharp breaks in it were between the *caciques* and the rest of the free population, and between the free population and the slaves. The position of the *caciques*, however, was an ever-weakening one. Most of them had lost their wealth in dealings with the Spaniards, and those who remained in power were very much Hispanicized and effectively as creole as most of the Spaniards of colonial birth.

THE REPUBLICAN AND EARLY MODERN PERIOD (1820–1910)

The remnants of authority held by the *caciques* constituted a thorn in the side of any group attempting to establish a centralized government, and one of the first moves of the republican government was to destroy the legal basis of the *caciques'* superiority. At the same time, it eliminated the elaborate colonial legal scheme of ethno-racial distinctions in an effort to make all Peruvians equal before the law. The last change was a long, drawn-out process and did not become effective in matters such as ecclesiastical organization until about 1900. The basis of the new government was theoretically democratic; except for the slaves, all citizens were equal in the eyes of the law, and distinctions of birth had been erased. Payment of taxes was a duty of all free citizens, and the burdens of obligatory labor (as in postal service) were supposed to fall equally on the shoulders of all free Peruvians. In fact, the state was an oligarchy, just as it had been before, except that some of the protective features of colonial law no longer applied to the privileged class of *caciques*. As a result, the Indians were in a weaker position than before; regardless of the legal provisions of the new constitution (and later ones), they continued to supply corvée labor for some purposes until the 1920's. The peasant estate had become a proletariat.

In Ica the highest stratum of society was composed of influential creoles. The wealthiest of these spent most of their time in Lima, jockeying for position in the national hierarchy and leaving effective control of the valley to a lesser class, the provincial gentry. Below the provincial gentry there was a major break in the social structure, on the other side of which existed the remainder of the population. That mass, in the early republican period, consisted of about three classes — peasants, landless laborers, and, below another major gap, the slaves. Both political and economic power followed the same chain of patronage through the society from a focus in the upper class.

The system was not to retain these specific characteristics for long, however. Three changes occurred between the 1850's and the turn of the century. First, a trickle of European immigrants, largely Italians, began coming into the valley just before mid-century and swelled to a sizeable flow after 1875. Second, the slaves were granted total emancipation in 1855, and third, there was a relatively minor stream of Asiatic immigration from the 1850's to about 1870, when Chinese bond servants were being imported to replace the diminishing numbers of slaves.

The changes which occurred because of emancipation and the Asiatic traffic were relatively simple. The freed Negroes joined the lower stratum of landless laborers; some of them entered into sharecropping contracts with landowners, and the remainder worked as wage laborers. There were differences in social standing between Negroes and Indian peasants, but mestization had proceeded and continued to proceed so rapidly that those were soon erased. The Chinese held a low status while they were in bondage, comparable to that previously held by the Negroes, but when released they, too, entered the lower levels of the population. Most of them set up small businesses and gradually moved upward in the social scale; others entered into ramified cooperative contracts on rural estates and made considerable profits. Generally speaking, their numbers were small and they had little effect on the social system as a whole.

The changes brought about by the European immigration were more complex and far-reaching in effect, for the new Europeans did not simply add themselves to one end of the structure as the Negroes or Chinese did, but entered it in the middle and grossly upset the preexistent system. Further, although they were probably not more numerous than the Chinese, they entered the structure at a point which had a low total population; they were thus able to achieve a much greater effect. Some of the Italians were men of great wealth and influence who assumed positions similar to those of the wealthy creoles. Others were of lesser standing and mingled with the provincial gentry. The remainder, particularly those railroad laborers who had come in after the completion of the Ica–Pisco line in 1875, were relatively poor but industrious and desirous of bettering their position. Most important of all, they did not fit the system. Up to this time, almost all Europeans had been persons of wealth and influence; now there were relatively large numbers of Europeans who were little better off than the wealthier peasants, but who could not be classed with them. The net effect of the Italian immigration was to begin to fill the chasm between the upper and the lower classes and provide the lowest of the Italians with strong ties of minority identification to some persons of great wealth and influence. The wealthy Italians displaced some of the influential Spaniards to positions in the class of provincial gentry, the Italians of lesser wealth pushed some of the provincial gentry out into the no-man's-land below the upper class, where the remainder of the Italians joined them. In short, there was created a kind of upper middle class in which the chain of patronage and control was slightly different from that of the earlier system, since the Italians tended to assist each other in their affairs. These phenomena were largely urban, however, so that it is necessary to describe the class systems of the country and city separately for the turn of the century.

In the country there was an upper class of wealthy creoles who were seldom present but controlled their lands through renters or let them to sharecroppers. Below them, and in practical control, were the provincial gentry, who owned smaller properties (ca. 15– 150 hectares). Then, after a relatively wide social gap, came peasants with 3–10 hectares of land and the more successful sharecroppers and renters. Below them were lesser sharecroppers and renters and finally the landless laborers. In the city the two upper classes were similar and composed of almost the same people, but they were followed in the scale by a rapidly expanding class of businessmen and shopkeepers, the upper middle class of which we spoke above. Below them were the smaller *mestizo* and Chinese businessmen and then the urban laborers, composed of Indians, *mestizos*, and Negroes. In both urban and rural areas, any highland Indians occupied a position below that of the local population.

THE LATE MODERN PERIOD (1910–1957)

There are two striking differences between the class structure of modern Ica and that of the turn of the century. First, the rural gentry have practically disappeared. Only a few persons of upper-class status live in the country now, and they are individuals of great wealth who also spend a good deal of their time in Lima. There are, however, some relatively wealthy owners in the country who would fit best into the category of upper middle class; they are what remains of the lower stratum of the provincial gentry. The remainder of their fellows can afford to maintain residences in Ica or Lima and do so. Second, there has arisen a great class of urban employees — secretaries, bookkeepers, skilled industrial laborers — whose standing is below that of the upper middle class but still superior to that of the remainder of the urban population.

They constitute what could be called the lower middle class.[6]

In the city, political power rests largely in the hands of the upper class — the descendants of the wealthy creoles and Italians of the early 1900's. The Italians among them hold most of the local economic power but not all of the political power, because of the advantage still held by the Spaniards on grounds of traditionally superior social position. The uppermost stratum of society is somewhat more active in provincial affairs than before, since modern transportation methods make it possible for its members to pay more attention to those local happenings which affect their standing. Most of the members of this upper class commute constantly between Ica and Lima.

The urban upper middle class is composed largely of businessmen of medium income, engineers, lawyers, and other professionals. Most of them are of European background, and the number of persons of Italian descent is high. It is from the boundary between this class and the upper that the *alcaldes* of the city come. Most other positions of influence in the political structure are also filled by members of the upper middle class — *concejales* (or *regidores*, councilmen), directors of government offices, and the more influential instructors in the secondary schools.[7]

The lower middle class of the city is considerably below the upper middle class in standing, so that the social gulf of the republican period is far from closed. Individuals of the lower middle class are usually of mixed descent and rural origin. They have no

[6] Although the distinction between manual and nonmanual occupations is an important one, the distinction between executive and nonexecutive occupations is even more important. Thus, secretaries are not classed with junior executives, and skilled workers are higher than unskilled, even though they work with their hands.

[7] All of these offices are appointive. The chief governmental officer of the Department of Ica is the prefect, appointed from Lima. He is usually a Limeño and a member of the upper middle class there. Below him is a subprefect with authority over the province, the *alcalde* of the city of Ica, who is also *alcalde* of the province, the *alcaldes* of the district capitals, and the *gobernadores* and *teniente-gobernadores* of progressively smaller villages. There are, in addition, justices of the peace and members of the Civil Guard (uniformed police). The line of police authority runs from the prefect, the subprefect, and *gobernador* down to the *teniente-gobernador* and ultimately to the Civil Guard. The *alcalde* is an administrative official without police authority, although he may request police aid from the appropriate official at his own level. The justices of the peace are responsible to the Superior Court of Ica.

political power in the city as individuals, even though some of them may be influential in their own home villages or in voluntary associations such as football clubs or labor unions.[8] They are almost all salaried employees (*empleados*), even if engaged in industrial trades, and their ability to accumulate wealth is severely limited by their lack of invested capital.

The lower class of the city is composed of a mass of wage laborers, many of whom are of highland origin or ancestry. They have no political influence in the overall social scheme as individuals and seldom organize to provide a mass basis for the making of public policy. Below them in the scale come the recent unacculturated migrants from the sierra, practically a caste apart, who may speak little or no Spanish, whose women wear highland costume, and who perform the most menial of the urban occupations, such as those of sweepers, porters, waiters, and casual laborers.[9]

The situation in the country is somewhat different. The uppermost stratum is identical in membership with the upper class in the city. The upper middle class is practically identical with that of the city, although there are some individuals in it who live in the rural area instead of the urban. These upper- and upper-middle-class people are all *hacendados* in the local terminology; the wealthiest of them control from 50 to 3000 hectares of land, and the less wealthy at least 15. Members of the upper class have much direct influence in the countryside if they live there, although it is unofficial. They do not participate in rural government. Members of the upper middle class rarely take part in rural government

[8] In 1956, many of them were supporters of the Alianza Popular Revolucionaria Americana, but by 1962 their support may have swung to the Acción Popular of Belaúnde, perhaps for reasons of geographical loyalty. See Patch 1966.

[9] The lower lower class of the city of Ica comprised about 900 persons in 1956, or under 3 percent of the city population. In the 1961 census, the *same* quarters of the city held at least 3000 persons, or about 7 percent of the city population. All the areas listed in the census as *barriadas* (slums) held almost 8000 persons, or 19 percent of the city population. Comparisons between the urban slums and a rural village in 1956 showed that the slum dwellers had fewer lineal and more lateral kinship ties, more nonkinship ties, a higher frequency of matricentrically organized families, and in general exhibited greater rootlessness and more severe results of economic pressure and proletarization. The increase in the percentage of slum dwellers by 1961 may indicate an intensification of these pressures. See Hammel 1961, 1964a, and for comparative materials Lewis 1959, 1961, 1965; Mangin 1960, 1967.

Top, *peasant women of the lower class in San Juan;* bottom, *highland women selling fruit in the city.*

and then only as *alcaldes* of district capitals. Those of them who do even that are looked down upon by their fellows for participating in the affairs of the *cholos* (peasants).

The gap between the upper middle and lower middle classes in the country is similar to that in the city; it is one between a "white" and a "nonwhite" population, although the racial and implied ethnic differences are not consistently distributed on either side of the gap. The lower middle class is composed of peasants who have enough land to live on without working for wages and of some employees of local haciendas or of the government. Below them comes a lower class, some members of which have tiny parcels of land, but who must work for wages in order to support their families. Last come the migrant highland laborers who work for the great haciendas, forming a lower lower class as they do in the city. *Alcaldes* and other rural officials come from the lower middle class (except as noted above), as do the leaders of voluntary associations. The lower class has little political authority and the lower lower none at all.[10]

The major gaps in the social system now lie between the upper middle class and the lower middle class, and between the lower and the lower lower classes. This is, in essence, the same system as that which existed in republican times, although the specific membership has changed. The most important change has been the gradual enlargement of the lower middle class of the city, which existed only in embryonic form in the 1850's. There is still a wide economic gap between these skilled employees and the employers and professionals who form the class above them — their social status is much lower, and their political influence as individuals minor. Nevertheless, when they act in concert, as during the strikes of bank employees and truck drivers in 1958, they exhibit an increasing degree of political power and awareness of its potentialities. They are becoming a force with which upper-class politicians must reckon directly and not simply through a chain of patronage.

[10] An analysis of the dimensions of social ranking in the village of San Juan Bautista in 1957 showed that the most important variables were the occupations of nonfarmers and the amounts of land worked by farmers. See Hammel 1962b. For comparative discussion of race and class relationships see Adams 1953; Gillin 1960; Harris 1964; Hohenthal 1959; Wagley 1963, 1965.

CHAPTER SEVEN

Style
of Life

THE HUMAN APPROACH

Prestige is a much more difficult variable to deal with than economic or even than political power. It is more difficult intrinsically, because it is harder to measure, and more difficult to describe historically, because its independent distribution through the social structure in times past is poorly specified. In order to describe the history and current nature of status honor in Ica, I must abandon an explicitly historical approach and revert to that reconstructionism which has always been the splintered crutch of anthropology. In the pages following, I present a series of vignettes on the styles of life of segments of the social hierarchy of modern Ica. These serve as a kind of comparative anatomy of status honor, the end results of a process whose major outlines have already been set forth through the social paleontology of economic and political history. The analogy is not idly made, for I assume that the processes of change in social prestige are like those which occur in the perishable parts of species, parallel to those which may be gleaned from examination of the more durable evidence of change in economic and political arrangements. Further, I regard prestige behavior somewhat more as the symbol of structures of wealth and authority and less as an independent distributive system.[1]

There are other reasons for this methodological compromise. An ethnographer can learn about wealth, power, and technology by observing large numbers of people in his subject culture and by reading written reports. As a result, his generalizations are wide, and most of the people he considers are relatively anonymous; the Iquenian in previous chapters has been a kind of generalized inhabitant of the valley. On the other hand, an ethnographer learns about the details of family life, medicine, religion, and personal attitudes through close and intimate observation. His sample, consequently, is smaller but more human, and the Iquenians in this chapter are very real people. Since my knowledge of the less technological and formal aspects of Ica society is derived from acquaintance with a few people, I prefer to discuss these aspects of social class largely in terms of individuals. What follows, then, is a series of personal sketches of people reasonably typical of their social classes. (Their names, of course, are fictitious, and the labels for the social classes are but convenient categorizations on a continuum of status.) Where their behavior is atypical, it will be noted, and where my observations of them are insufficient to describe the behavior of the social class to which they belong, they will be supplemented by drawing on other, similar individuals. Finally, those aspects of their behavior which are of major historical importance in this study will be noted.

THE UPPER CLASS

I

Enrique Soldán comes from an old and respected family of Spanish descent. The hacienda which he operates as part of the family

---

[1] For discussion of the nature of change in prestige behavior and its general tendency to proceed downward in social hierarchies, see Fallers 1954; Hammel 1964b; Tarde 1895. For general background on Peruvian "culture" see Carrera Vergara 1954; Fuentes 1866; Martínez Compañón 1936; Means 1918; Patrón 1935; Prince 1890; Pursche 1944; Simmons 1955b; Wright 1908.

corporation has been in their hands since the early 1800's, although it was operated under absentee renting contracts until about 1940. Like most upper-class persons, he has a pride of lineage and a sense of history which validate his claim to wealth and position, characteristics lacking in the lower classes.[2]

The Soldán family is atypical in its residence pattern, since its members spend much more time on their farm than do most members of the upper class. Enrique is there almost constantly, but his wife and children spend about three-quarters of the year in Lima where the children are in private school. The Soldáns have a house in Lima, and Enrique travels back and forth to Lima during the school year, spending a long weekend with his family and the rest of the week on the farm. His commuting would have been impossible before the advent of the automobile and the Pan-American Highway. In the old days he would have had his choice between a life as an isolated although successful farmer and one as an absentee landlord who paid little attention to his property. Now he can take the best of both possibilities.

The Soldán farmhouse is spacious and well furnished, of whitewashed adobe and concrete with flagstone floors. Its appointments are simple, almost rustic, and exhibit the Soldáns' restrained taste. The atmosphere is "proper Bostonian" more than anything else and is typical of most of the life of the Soldáns. The house itself would be worth about $60,000 in the United States, without considering the offices, farm buildings, and servants' quarters which are close by.

On the farm, Enrique dresses in cotton khaki trousers, jodhpur boots, a white shirt open at the throat, and a straw hat. This costume is different only in detail from what a wealthy farmer would have worn a generation ago, when riding breeches and high boots were the rule. Sra. Soldán wears simple cotton housedresses of American cut at home; they are more casual than the severe black and gray dresses that Enrique's mother used to wear. When Enrique goes to the city on business he usually changes to wool trousers and discards the hat. If his affairs will keep him in the city until dinner time, he changes to coat and tie. On formal oc-

[2] Cf. Hammel 1964b; Strickon 1962.

66

casions the Soldáns wear the same kind of clothes that would be worn by members of the American upper or upper middle class. The children are similarly attired; on the farm they wear cotton clothes but don finer garments on formal occasions.

The Soldáns own several farm vehicles as well as a late model Chevrolet for their own use. Enrique says that some of his friends have chided him about the Chevrolet, remarking that he should own a more luxurious car. He discussed the implications of this situation with me in a roundabout way, pointing out that he is perfectly able to buy a fancier car but simply dislikes ostentation. He is scornful of the new rich in Ica, who display their wealth with expensive cars (often several to a family), luxurious clothes, and high living.

Enrique was educated in Lima and at a university in the United States. He was one of the first of his generation to attend a college in the United States; most of his predecessors studied in France or Germany.[3] His wife was educated in Europe, during her family's residence there. Both of them are fond of classical music, European art, and books, and they speak frequently of the concerts and exhibits they have seen in Lima. Enrique's interest in intellectual matters, particularly in history, is not unusual among members of the upper fringe of the upper class; some of his fellows devote much of their time to historical investigations and have published works on local history. Most of these efforts are far from professional, but they indicate a strong inclination toward amateur and gentlemanly scholarly activity.

The simple but expensive tastes of the family are also evident in their diet. Meat is served at almost every meal, and the dishes are more American or European in style than Peruvian. The common Peruvian soup which includes all the scraps in the kitchen is never served, and highly spiced creole dishes are rare. The family eats relatively little by contrast with most Peruvians, although there is enough on the table for everyone. All the members of the family eat together and are served by the single house servant, a butler,

[3] Education in the United States is now common. The former President of Peru (Belaúnde) studied architecture at the University of Texas. Most wealthy Peruvians go to southern universities, perhaps for reasons which will be obvious below.

who also does the cleaning and cooking. When wine is served at dinner, it is a dry table wine of European type, not the sweet fortified wine of the countryside. If Enrique offers his guests a drink, it is most likely to be a Martini, bourbon, or Scotch.

Most of the Soldáns' social activities center in Lima, where they visit at the homes of friends or meet at the Club Nacional, the most prestigious social club in Peru. Enrique is proud of his membership, although he refers to it only obliquely. He attends social functions in Ica but rarely. If these are private affairs, they are at the homes of social equals or in the upper-class club of Ica, the Centro Social. Enrique usually goes to the Centro only for his haircuts. On the rare occasions when he participates in a public dinner, he goes to the Unión Social Ica, the middle-class club, which doubles as a community center. When he visits the city about once a week on business he may have coffee or a drink with a friend in the upper-class hotel, the Colón, where he also has supper when business keeps him late in the city. He does not go to the middle-class hotel and bar, the Trocadero, although he will converse over coffee with middle-class acquaintances at another restaurant, Navarro's.

Life in the Soldán household and the relationships between its members are quiet and restrained. Sra. Soldán has a great deal of authority in the management of the house and often asks her husband to run errands for her in the city. The children are well behaved, quiet, but firmly disciplined. Sra. Soldán spends much time with them, teaching them to read and to play various games. There are no other members of the family in the household besides the two adults and the children, although they are sometimes visited by relatives from Lima. The butler is the only house servant, but there are many others who are concerned with the farm and who take care of the grounds. Enrique also has a chauffeur to drive him on long trips; he says, deprecatingly, that he tends to fall asleep at the wheel and would rather have someone else drive.

Enrique and his wife are deeply religious; they attend church in Lima or Ica, and Enrique sometimes contributes to the major expenses of the cathedral in Ica. They do not participate in the traditional religious celebrations of the valley, however, and Enrique has never even seen the great processions at Yauca in September or at Luren in October and Holy Week. The Soldáns do have one traditional celebration on their farm, however — the feast of the hacienda's patron saint, which all the employees attend. The festival is the occasion for marriages and christenings and is presided over by the Soldáns and a cleric of rather high ecclesiastical rank whom they invite from Lima.

When someone in the family is sick, he goes to the doctor. In an emergency he would be taken to a physician in Ica, but the regular family doctor is in Lima. Sra. Soldán is skilled in first aid and nursing and takes care of many of these things herself. On Sundays she often tends to the sick children of the farm employees, advising them to go to the doctor, under the government health insurance program, if she cannot help them herself. In their own home the Soldáns pay no attention to the traditional differences between "hot" and "cold" foods which were introduced by their Spanish ancestors, nor do they attempt many folk cures, other than those which involve simple remedies for stomachaches and minor ailments.[4]

The Soldáns are the godparents of many of the farm workers' children and thus stand in *compadre* relationship to many of their employees. In addition, they are *padrinos* of marriage to many of the workers.[5] Most of the permanent employees are Negroes, descendants of the hacienda's slaves, and the relationship between them and the hacienda house is particularly close. When some of the old workmen have difficulties with officials or businessmen

[4] The characteristics of heat and cold, widely applied to foods in Latin America, have nothing to do with their temperatures but with innate "medical" qualities derived from the ancient Hippocratic humoral classification of hot or cold and wet or dry. Currier posits a relationship between social insecurity and continued adherence to traditional hot-cold distinctions (1966). Functionally, he may be correct, and the relationship probably extends to beliefs in *susto* (fright), *mal ojo* (evil eye), and other "supernatural" ills. Historically, both inadequate economic and political position and continued adherence to such medical practices are the result of delayed transmission of cultural benefits and attitudes from the elite to the lower strata.

[5] For a description of the complexity of *compadrazgo* relationships in Peru see Gillin 1947a. Mintz and Wolf place these relationships in the historical context of changing European society (1950), and Foster relates them to the generic form of dyadic contracts (1963). A general discussion is contained in Eisenstadt 1956; Foster 1953c.

in the city, Enrique intercedes for them. He also lends them money and assists them in other ways. In return, they are trustworthy employees and faithful to the family. The pattern of *compadrazgo* between owner and workmen, with its paternalistic coloring, was more common in Ica in former years than it is now.

These are some of the more visible aspects of Enrique's life. There are others, however, which illustrate his personal attitudes even more clearly. He dislikes most of the people in the valley on the grounds that "they are not gentlemen." He is amazed at their ostentatious behavior and scandalized by the provocative creole dress styles of their women, even though he sometimes managed a wink at me when a particularly attractive girl passed. His disdain has been tacitly communicated even to his butler, who, announcing to Enrique that several wealthy Italians had just driven up, once said, ". . . *han llegado Vanesso y Picardi*," omitting the usual title of *Señor* from their names (". . . Vanesso and Picardi have arrived"). Enrique is active in local politics on a high level, and much of his effort is devoted to thwarting the economic and political aspirations of the Italian *nouveaux riches*, who now control most of the valley. On the other hand, Enrique likes Americans and Englishmen. He is friendly with the upper-class representatives of a large American company in Ica, with a wealthy American, and with an English farmer. His upbringing and education make him feel more at home with people who adhere to American or British upper-class or upper-middle-class standards.

Enrique is the epitome of *noblesse oblige*, even to the meanest highlander. When he orders food in a restaurant or gives instructions to a workman, for example, he always prefaces his command with, "Do me the favor . . . ." If some of his more experienced workmen think that a decision regarding farm work is in error, they will not hesitate to give him their advice, and he often accepts it. He is so flexible in this respect that it would seem to a more authoritarian individual or to one with greater status anxiety that he lacked the ability to be a firm leader and that his employees took advantage of him. Nevertheless, the efficiency of his labor force is much higher than that of most in the valley. In his own way he persuades the men to do their jobs well.

70

Enrique regards his workers in a benevolent but condescending way. He is sometimes surprised by their intelligence or their importance in their own social spheres. His butler, for example, comes from a small village in the upper Ica canyon where he is an important personage. During the year, villagers often come to the hacienda to seek the advice or assistance of the butler. Enrique thinks it paradoxical that his butler should be a man of such importance. On another occasion, he mentioned to me that his chauffeur owned two automobiles and employed drivers to operate them as long-distance *colectivos* (taxis with fixed routes); Enrique thought this extraordinary. He prefers Negroes to local workers or highlanders, saying that the Negroes are superior. Furthermore, he likes to use the Negroes as foremen, since they keep apart from the highlanders who form the bulk of his field labor. Enrique doubts if even education and training can overcome the "indifference, laziness, and retarded mental condition" of most of the Indians.

Enrique's attitudes are typical of the *gran patrón*, but it is doubtful if any *hacendado* of the past ever adhered to them more closely than he does now.[6] Enrique acts as he does from a sense of high social position and moral responsibility to the lower classes, and from an infusion of American or British ideas on the proper style of living which are somewhat more puritanical than those of his fellow Peruvians. His attitudes are not unusual among members of the very top of Peruvian society, but they are different from those of the typical members of the upper class, many of whom do precisely the things of which Enrique disapproves.

II

At the lower fringe of the upper class, we may consider the behavior of Emilio Gutiérrez. His father was a member of the provincial gentry and a minor political official; Emilio now holds an important political post in Ica. The family tradition is one of impetuous and forceful behavior. Once, when Emilio's father found that an administrator of an irrigation ditch had diverted water to another farm without consulting him, he mounted his

[6] Cf. Foster 1961, 1963; Gillin 1960:36–38; Kenny 1960; Romano 1960.

horse and whipped the unfortunate man several kilometers into the city. The old man left property to his sons, but they lost it in unwise speculation. Finally, Emilio used his political influence to obtain a contract in the channelling of the river and within a short time had amassed enough money to start farming again. He married the daughter of a local country gentleman and was fortunate in getting an influential and wealthy man as his *padrino* of marriage. The *padrino* lent him enough money to buy a good farm and dig one of the first tubular wells in Ica. Emilio's success at cotton farming and selling water has made him a wealthy man. He rents, rather than owns, most of his farmland, however, and all his money is spent on capital improvement, rapid expansion, and luxury display, so that he must finance his farming operations through loans from the cotton gins. A few years ago he owed 3,000,000 soles ($150,000) to one of the gins, and they have since refused to give him more credit, even though the debt has been paid.

The Gutiérrez house is about the same size as Soldán's but different in style. It is a modern copy of the hacienda house that was popular in the 1800's, raised about three meters from ground level, with a veranda running all along the front, and forming one side of a square of buildings. The other buildings are garages, storehouses, and offices of the hacienda. The house is of adobe and concrete, has concrete floors, and cost about the same as the Soldán home. It is more sumptuously furnished and not at all rustic in appearance.

The dress of the Gutiérrez family is not different from that of the Soldáns, except that the mature, unmarried daughters wear tighter, more provocative clothes. Most of these are similar to the clothes worn by actresses in French and Italian movies; tight black toreador pants and blouses are particularly favored by girls of the upper and upper middle classes.[7] Emilio appears frequently in his shirtsleeves in the city, although he changes to coat and tie on more formal occasions. His adult son is often seen in the same attire, but with a large straw hat to which he is inseparably attached. The Gutiérrez' own several pickup trucks and a late model

[7] Miniskirts were not yet in style.

72

Housing in the Ica Valley: top, *a traditional hacienda with the distillery in the foreground;* middle, *a street in San Juan, showing a traditional village house at the far end of the street, with "modern" houses in the foreground;* bottom, *houses of the lower class, with the author's car in the foreground (see page xi).*

car. The father usually drives the car, and the son takes one of the pickups.

Emilio was educated in Ica, as was his wife. The son has attended Peruvian schools and also spent a year in the United States, studying agriculture at a small college in California. He did not finish his courses there because of language difficulties and speaks almost no English now. The daughters go to the public secondary school in Ica; that is atypical for their class, but Emilio has so many children that he cannot afford to send them all to private school. None of the family expresses any interest in classical music, books, or art, or in the indigenous art of Peru. The eldest son is fond of modern American and Latin American dance music and hopes to purchase a high-fidelity phonograph and collect records. This lack of individual artistic expression and intellectual activity is common among Gutiérrez' fellows in Ica now, but it contrasts with the pattern among the provincial gentry in past years. A generation or two ago many country gentlemen wrote novels, poetry, or folkloristic descriptions of the countryside, and some discussion of these matters was common at the frequent hacienda parties of the time. Some of these efforts were excellent, as the short stories of Valdelomar illustrate, and some less so, like the writings of the Caso brothers, but they existed. Nowadays there is a little bad history written and nothing more; most intellectual activity is carried on by persons of very high status and usually in urban surroundings.

The Gutiérrez family eats more, on the average, than the Soldáns do. They also serve more traditional Peruvian foods, such as soups and highly spiced dishes. Emilio and his son eat alone in the dining room, and his wife and other children eat in a crowded small room to one side, a pattern more typical of the lower classes. If Emilio drinks wine, it is a table wine, and if he takes liquor, it is usually whiskey. He rarely drinks *pisco*, and then it is usually in a mixed drink such as a *pisco* sour.

Emilio's political position makes him somewhat more active in local social affairs than other members of the upper class. He belongs to the Centro Social, visits it frequently, and also presides

74

over many community affairs in the Unión Social Ica. The son also belongs to the Centro and is quite proud of the fact. He frequents the Hotel Colón, the Trocadero, and the bars of the resort hotels in Huacachina. The family entertains relatively little in their country home, departing from the old pattern of inter-hacienda visiting, and many of their social activities take place in Lima. Emilio has political as well as social connections in Lima and often goes there to make arrangements in his capacity as a local governing official.

Emilio is much sterner in family matters than Enrique Soldán, as one might gather from his habit of eating apart from his wife and children. He also follows the common practice of conducting many of his social relationships without his wife; only a few close friends are ever entertained or visited by both adults. Sra. Gutiérrez has a great deal to say about the running of the household, but final authority rests with her husband; he would never think of running errands for her. Relationships between Emilio and his wife may be somewhat strained; it is said that the old man keeps a mistress in the city. The eldest son clashes frequently with his father, especially since Emilio turned over management of the farm to him. The boy feels that his father continues to interfere, and he dislikes his advice. The two argue incessantly about everything imaginable. On the other hand, the son is devoted to his mother and very protective toward his sisters. He regards himself in many ways as the man of the house and the protector of its female members.

The religious practices of the Gutiérrez family conform more closely to the valley norm than do those of the Soldáns. Last year Emilio's brother walked fifteen kilometers to the festival at Yauca in fulfillment of a vow, hoping to rid himself of a heart condition. Emilio does not belong to any local *mayordomía*; those activities have always been the province of the lower classes. While religious curing by vows to the Virgin or the saints is not uncommon among Emilio's fellows, they never consult lay curers and seldom use home remedies unless they come from the drugstore. All major illnesses are treated by a physician.

75

Both Emilio and his son are emphatic in their attitude that they are as good as or better than anyone in the valley. They are both forceful and authoritarian men. Emilio is regarded as a stern but just employer by his workers, and a good *patrón*, but the son is hated by most of them. Emilio will grant favors and act as *padrino* at their weddings, particularly if the workman has been with him for a long time, but the boy will have none of this. He refers to the peasants as *bestias* (beasts) or *cholos de mierda* (peasants of excrement), although he refrains from using these terms in their presence. When he gives orders to a foreman, the son is haughty and imperious; he looks through the workman or past him, delivers his commands in an icy tone, and then drives off without waiting for a reply.[8] The men tremble at his approach. I lost the confidence of many small peasants when I became friendly with Emilio's son, so little do they trust him. They phrase their dislike of him in terms of his departure from the ideal behavior of a *patrón*; he is not a *"gran patrón"* like his father, they say, but a *"malcriado"* (spoiled child).[9]

Emilio's acquaintances point out that the Gutiérrez family was once in severe economic straits and has improved only because of Emilio's incessant energy. They suggest that the harsh attitude which the son displays toward the workmen stems from his fear of economic insecurity and his remembrance of the family's near-peasant economic status at one time. A sense of inferiority and a desire to compensate for it does run through much of what the eldest son does. Emilio is typical of the members of the provincial gentry who have continued in their agricultural occupations but have improved their economic positions and entered vigorously into local political life. Emilio is a powerful, influential, and ruthless man who has risen to eminence through a combination of his own efforts and political connections. Like most *caudillos* (political bosses), he is respected for his power by other members of

[8] In asking a child where her father was, his phrase was *"¿Que hay de tu papá?"* or, affectively translated, "Where the hell is your old man?" Enrique Soldán would have said, *"¿Donde está tu papá?"*

[9] Literally, "badly brought up." See Lauria 1964:55 on demeanor.

the upper class, but despised for his origins. To some of them, he is a *cholo cargado de plata* (a cholo with a lot of money).

THE UPPER MIDDLE CLASS

III

Giuseppe Bologna is a Peruvian-born member of an influential Italian family which administers a large agricultural property in the valley. He himself has no part in the operation of the farm but gains his livelihood as local agent for a large Peruvian commercial company. This business is the last in a series of small ventures he has pursued all over South America.

Giuseppe is married but has no household in Ica. His wife is a teacher in a private school in Lima and lives there with their adolescent son. During the week, Giuseppe lives in a room in the Trocadero and takes his meals in the hotel dining room. On weekends he visits Lima or stays with his brothers on the farm. When his wife visits him in Ica about once a month, they stay either at the hotel or at the farm. Giuseppe plans to borrow money from one of his brothers and get a house or apartment in Luren, the middle-class residential district of the city. The homes there are built along modern American lines, and most of them are very similar in style to houses in the $25,000 to $30,000 class in Southern California. The architecture is often a modernized Spanish colonial. The newer homes are furnished in North American middle-class style, and the ladies of the neighborhood frequently consult magazines such as *House Beautiful* or *House & Garden* for suggestions on how to decorate.

Giuseppe dresses more formally than upper-class men of the rural area because he is almost always in the city. Instead of khaki pants and white shirt, he has gabardine trousers and a sport shirt as casual attire. Sometimes he puts on a sport jacket and a cocky beret and is really a dapper fellow, but he rarely wears a tie. Sra. Bologna wears the kinds of dresses that would be selected by a North American woman for going downtown; they are of solid colors and conservative cuts which befit her ample, middle-aged figure. The Bolognas had no car until recently, and Giuseppe used

77

to borrow his brother's jeep. A short time ago he bought a European military-type vehicle of which he is very fond. Giuseppe likes jeeps and other overland vehicles because he uses them to visit archaeological sites; he is an inveterate pot-hunter.

Both adult Bolognas have had Peruvian educations, but neither is a university graduate. Giuseppe is much interested in photography, modern art, and antiquities but indulges his interests in some of these fields in a commercial fashion, which is something his brothers would never do. They regard archaeological specimens, for example, as curiosities which a person of wealth and education can afford to collect and admire. Many people of urban upper-class and upper-middle-class status have a similar attitude toward the arts. Some of them are sufficiently interested in matters of local history to assemble old documents and publish the results of their research, and a few of them paint in oils, model clay, or write occasional bits of poetry. Little of this work could be regarded as "good" within the general canons of European art; it is a hobby to most practitioners, and they follow it only sporadically and as a means of enhancing their local prestige.

Giuseppe does not belong to the Centro Social, nor does he frequent the Unión Social. Most of his activities in Ica center around the Trocadero, although his brothers would never enter it. He takes all his meals there and delights in the highly spiced foods which are served; they are a part of the local folklore which he enjoys so much. He takes morning coffee in the Colón and afternoon refreshment at a middle-class ice cream parlor or at Navarro's coffee shop. Both upper- and lower-middle-class persons go to the ice cream parlor, and upper-class persons such as Soldán sometimes drop into Navarro's to talk to their upper-middle-class acquaintances. Most of Giuseppe's equals have more active social lives in Ica, centering around the Unión Social, the Trocadero, or the resort hotels in Huacachina.

The Bolognas are Roman Catholics, like most Iquenians, but they do not participate in the major religious festivals of the valley. Few Italians do. However, Giuseppe likes to photograph these events, which he regards as an interesting bit of local folklore. He attends church regularly and gives alms with a pious air to every beggar who approaches him. Giuseppe is a sick man, but he never seeks a cure by religious means or at the hands of lay curers. He either goes to the doctor or ministers to himself with medicines from the drugstore. His hypochondriac tendencies have made him quite an expert on home medication, and he is full of advice on what to use for heart trouble, dysentery, and athlete's foot.

Giuseppe considers himself a man of the world — independent, knowledgeable, and debonair. In reality, he is dominated by most of his relatives. His elder brother, who is almost unbelievably opinionated, moulds Giuseppe's thinking and is the source of most of the pronouncements on art, morality, and politics that Giuseppe utters so wisely over his coffee. His wife is a strong-willed woman, and Giuseppe usually defers to her. Many of the stories he tells of his sexual exploits have an undertone of wishful rebellion in them. His is a difficult position; he is looked down upon by his successful brothers and their equals, moves in a social class beneath them, yet struggles to maintain a position as a worldly, efficient businessman and a member of the upper class.

Giuseppe has a condescending attitude toward the natives of Ica, considering them much beneath him. He treats his employees with chilly reserve and seldom speaks to any other members of the lower classes. He has a few lower-class *compadres*; these are old servants of the family who have asked him to stand as godparent for their children. The godparents of his own son are relatives. In explaining his attitudes toward the peasants and highlanders, Giuseppe says that they are simple and childlike folk, poor, but basically honest. They need to be guided in this life by intelligent and sensitive persons like himself. He thinks that highland women are particularly praiseworthy; they are submissive, obedient, and one of the few types of women that can be "completely possessed by a man."

Although his "Walter Mitty" personality complicates matters a bit, Giuseppe is an excellent example of a provincial Peruvian urbanite. His interests and education are very much like those of the city-dwelling provincial gentry of the last generation, and he lives in the same social border zone between the upper and upper middle classes, high in the latter category but barred from the former because of his lack of personal wealth, some of his commercial dealings in art, and the middle-class restaurants he frequents.

Jorge Vasco comes from a family that has been in Ica for over a hundred years. His father owned a small hacienda which produced grapes, wine, and brandy; Jorge inherited the land a few years ago, added to it by purchase and rental, and replaced the vines with cotton. He has dug a well to irrigate the cotton, and even when his own fields have been watered, the big diesel roars constantly, pumping water for nearby peasants.

The Vasco house is about a hundred years old and built on the same general plan as that of Emilio Gutiérrez, who lives close by. Unlike the Gutiérrez house, it is of wood and adobe, poorly furnished, and somewhat shabby. The floors are of rough wood, sprayed with kerosene to keep the dust down, and the furniture is simple. The living room holds a glassed bookcase, a coffee table, and a few bamboo and rattan chairs. There is an upholstered couch in the next room, together with a few chairs, a small table, and a radio-phonograph. The dining room holds a large table and chairs of willow with reed seats, a sideboard, and a new refrigerator. The bedroom is crowded with a large, sagging bed for the adults, smaller beds for the young son and the two small daughters, and a crib for the baby. Jorge's recent success in cotton farming and the sale of well water have made it possible to paint the house, buy some new wicker furniture, put in new bathroom fixtures, and install a new electric washing machine. Sra. Vasco has bought some ornate wrought iron lamps for the living room and hopes eventually to remodel the whole house.

Around the farm Jorge dresses in khaki pants and a wrinkled shirt; he will wear the same clothes, often dirty, into the city if he goes himself to fetch barrels of diesel oil or construction materials. Otherwise, he dresses more neatly and will don coat and tie for formal occasions. He rarely shaves unless he goes into the city. Sra. Vasco wears simple cotton prints around the house but also dresses more formally for the city. The little girls dress in clean play clothes, and the boy is attired much like his father.

Jorge has an automobile about five years old and a second-hand truck which he uses for farm work. Both vehicles frequently need repair, and he looks longingly on some of the modern ranch wagons and new cars that wealthier farmers drive. Jorge is fascinated by automobiles and machinery in general. He is fortunate in owning both a truck and car; most farmers of his position have only a truck.

Both Vascos were educated in private schools in Lima; Sra. Vasco was born there. Jorge has the equivalent of a good high school education and knows a good deal of the botany, chemistry, and other sciences necessary to modern farming. He has little interest in intellectual activity and says he knows nothing of music or art. Sra. Vasco was amazed when my wife took her to an archaeological site in Ica and showed her the scraps of textiles and bits of broken pottery on the surface; she had read of the ancient cultures of Peru but never seen any of the local remains, even though Ica is one of the richest archaeological areas in Peru. Jorge loves to dance, and his taste runs to the modern North American rhythms or Latin American dances such as the tango or the *vals criollo*. He cannot dance the *marinera* which was popular in Ica in his grandfather's day among the provincial gentry and later among the local peasant class. It was introduced to Lima from France in the early 1800's and diffused rapidly down the social scale. Now it is popular only among the Indians of the sierra and some members of the upper class of Lima, where it has been reintroduced in a patriotically tinged folkloristic revival. Jorge's maids are from Córdova; he once asked them to demonstrate the *marinera* and the *huayno* (a typical highland dance) to my wife and me, and they performed with considerable skill. Jorge is also very fond of soccer (*fútbol*), which he used to play in school as a boy. He follows the national teams in the Lima newspapers and attends the larger matches in the city of Ica. He himself does not play any more; only the lower-class and lower-middle-class adult males of Ica participate in amateur soccer. If young men of the upper middle class form athletic teams, they play basketball or volleyball.

The Vascos' table is very much like that of their neighbors, the Gutiérrez'. Peruvian foods are common, and Sra. Vasco likes to prepare dishes heavily seasoned with coriander and chili peppers. Most of the cooking is done by her two maids, although she directs it. Jorge is fond of beer and some dry table wine but drinks little of the traditional fortified wine. He likes to offer whiskey to his guests when he can afford it; otherwise he serves *pisco*, usually mixed in a *pisco* Manhattan (*Capitán*). Sra. Vasco drinks very little.

Jorge and his wife complain that they have very little social life in Ica; they regard it, as do many middle-class people, as a stiff and unfriendly community where undue emphasis is placed on social prestige. Most of their social affairs are conducted in Lima with family and close friends. Sra. Vasco sometimes spends a few weeks at a time with her family there, and the family always visits Lima at least once a month. Despite their remarks about the unfriendly character of Ica, the Vascos visit their friends in the city and entertain them at their hacienda. Most of their acquaintances are minor professionals or administrators and their families. When the Vascos go to the city for entertainment, they visit the cinema, the Trocadero, or one of the popular *chifas*, which are the Peruvian version of a Chinese restaurant. Jorge would regard going to the Hotel Colón as a major event, like visiting the "Top of the Mark" in San Francisco. The Vascos are also visited by friends and kinsmen from Lima who often stay a week or so at the hacienda. The Limeños who come to their house are much like the Vascos, but slightly more "cityfied" in their dress and behavior. The women are usually dressed in tighter and more provocative clothes than Sra. Vasco wears — one-piece dresses of stylish cut for the older women and tights and blouses for the younger. The men wear wool or cotton sports clothes and seriously debate questions of economics and national government, which are matters that seldom concern Jorge when they are not present.

Jorge has some social activities in Ica, however, from which he excludes his wife. He is *bien criollo* (a real creole), or a "wolf" in North American terms, and often joins a male friend in town to pick up a streetwalker or, more rarely, visit a house of prostitution. Jorge feels that sexual intercourse with his wife is somewhat of a duty and that he must be concerned primarily with her delicate sensibilities as a respectable woman. If he wants to enjoy himself sexually, he goes to a lower-class woman or a prostitute, so that he can, in his words, "do anything." Sometimes he goes to a house of prostitution just to drink and dance, fearing disease if he has sexual relations with any of the women there; brothels are often frequented by men of the upper or upper middle class as nightclubs, and it is more common for the lower classes to engage the professional services of the ladies in them.

The Vasco household is a warm and affectionate one, if slightly hectic and disorganized. Jorge loves his wife and children deeply and is more demonstrative than most Peruvian men. His young son actively resents demonstrations of affection from his father, and the boy's attitude troubles Jorge, even though he says nothing about it. Everyone eats at the same table, where they are served by the maids from the adjoining kitchen. They may be joined by guests or even by a neighbor of slightly lower social status who works for Jorge as a part-time manager of the hacienda. Sra. Vasco has almost complete authority in the house, and Jorge accedes to all her demands.

In religious matters the Vascos do not differ much from others of their class or from people like Gutiérrez. They were married in church and attend mass faithfully each week. Sometimes they go to watch processions in the city, but it is more to let the children ride the Ferris wheel than to observe the religious aspect of a fiesta. In medical affairs, the Vascos refrain from visiting lay curers, saying that such customs are only for the ignorant and superstitious *cholos*. Most of Sra. Vasco's home remedies come from the pharmacy, although she sometimes makes a brew of herbs to cure a child's stomachache. They visit one of the more prominent physicians of Ica in minor or emergency cases but have most of their medical needs attended to in Lima.

Jorge's social relationships with the local peasants are relatively slight. He regards them as ignorant and untrustworthy in much the same way as young Gutiérrez does, although he does not have Gutiérrez' haughty air. Once, a proud and dignified old peasant came to the hacienda to protest Jorge's division of the water he was selling from the hacienda well, saying that he had requested it before a neighbor who was now irrigating. Jorge addressed him as "Don Carlos," was deferential because of the man's age, and granted his request. When the old man had gone, Jorge cursed him roundly, asking me if I knew how it was possible to do business when one had to deal with people like old Carlos. The Vascos have no *compadres* among the local population, although Sra. Vasco has contributed a few articles of costume to the peasant children who dance as "Negritos" before the various creches in village homes at Christmas time, thereby becoming the *madrina* (godmother) of the article she donated. Sra. Vasco remarked that having *compadres* among the peasants was more trouble than it was worth, for they always try to worm extra favors on the basis of the relationship. The Vascos' *compadres* are all in Lima, and most of them are kinsmen.

Jorge's social position exemplifies that of the provincial gentry who have remained in the rural area but have not risen in status like Gutiérrez. Most of their predecessors have given up country residence, and many have abandoned agriculture altogether. Jorge is forced by economic necessity to live on his land, and because he is a farmer, living without many of the conveniences of the city, his status is lower than that of most members of the upper middle class. Nevertheless, there is no doubt about his separateness from the peasants of the area, whom he regards as ignorant *cholos*. His maternal cousin, whose economic status is about the same as Jorge's, was recently appointed *alcalde* of a district capital; Jorge's feelings were mixed. He was envious of the political honor but shook his head sadly and said, "Look at him — he was a good boy, but now he is running around with all those *cholos*; he is almost a *cholo* himself." Although Jorge's living standards are close to those of the peasants in some ways, the social gap between them is very great.

THE LOWER MIDDLE CLASS

V

Pedro Romero is a peasant about forty years old who lives with his two young sons, a nephew, and his aged mother. His common-

Representatives of the middle classes: left, *a social equal of Jorge Vasco, from the upper middle class, with* botijas *in the background;* right, *a social equal of the Sorias, from the lower middle class.*

law wife left him a few years ago, and he shares the burden of housekeeping and cooking with his mother. As an illegitimate child unrecognized by his father, he has no inheritance other than his mother's house and land, which will go to him when she dies.

Common-law marriages, i.e., those sanctioned by neither church nor state, such as the one practiced by Pedro's parents and by himself and his former wife, constitute between a quarter and a third of all rural conjugal unions in the lower and lower middle classes. They are not looked down upon in a moral sense, although the woman's family always puts pressure on the man to formalize the union so that she will be economically secure. The frequency of such marriages in the past may have been higher, since certain modern legal requirements for birth certificates are often satisfied by the father's recognition of the child as his own on a civil marriage certificate, and the rate of civil marriages has thereby been stimulated. The rate of church marriages is still low (about 40 percent of the rural population), since they are too expensive for most peasants. Common-law marriages tend to be unstable, and families of abandoned wives and children are common. Pedro's case, in which the children remain with the father, is rare.[10]

The Romero house looks very much like Jorge Vasco's, although it is smaller, more crudely built, and raised only slightly above ground level. It has thick adobe walls, an adobe porch with a wooden roof, and glassless windows shuttered from within and barred with the traditional wooden grill (reja). The floors are of earth, pounded to concrete hardness by a half-century of sprinkling and the passage of many feet. Pedro is building a new house about fifty meters away. It, too, is of adobe but is more modern in plan. It has no porch or sunshade, but a small garden space in front, about two by four meters, enclosed by a concrete fence (chalet). This is a style of house introduced to the countryside from Lima and Ica about ten or twenty years ago. It will have shuttered windows but no grill, and concrete floors instead of earth. The house Pedro lives in now is typical of the older type of

[10] For comparisons of family structure between rural villages and urban slums see Hammel 1964a.

well-to-do peasant house in the village; the new one is the kind that replaced it. The old house has almost no furniture. A single, battered table stands in the front room, accompanied by two simple chairs. The bedrooms have iron cots, and the kitchen holds another table, some chairs, and a few shelves.

Pedro dresses in gabardine trousers and a shirt and wears shoes but no socks. He is a big man, but his pants are still two sizes too large. If he goes to town on a hot day, he simply changes into a clean version of what he is wearing. If it is cold, he may wear a suit jacket. He never wears a tie. His mother wears simple, ill-fitting cotton dresses around the house, as do most peasant women. These are either simple prints, such as a polka-dot pattern, or made of one color. The cut is loose and the neckline low. Sometimes the neckline is cut to the waist and fastened with buttons; a low neckline is much handier for women who breast-feed their children than a high neck or one which will not unbutton. Pedro's mother often wears her long hair in two braids, but the younger women of the village wear theirs short and in a "permanent." The boys in the house dress in khaki pants and shirts, the public school uniform introduced by the last governmental regime. The eldest boy wears shoes; the others are barefoot.

Pedro owns no car, but he has a donkey which he uses to carry various burdens around the farm. He can drive, however, and used to tell me with a humor he could not contain that if I would like to leave my old Model A with him overnight, it would be perfectly safe. Pedro is well educated for a peasant, and neighbors often call on him to read complicated legal papers or to draft petitions. When he was a boy he used to travel to Ica on horseback every day to attend the fourth and fifth grade (our fifth and sixth), taking his meals at the house of a friend in the city.[11] Many other peasant men have been through only the third grade (our fourth). Pedro remarks that anybody can get an education now, but before the busses started to run to Ica in 1925 it took a good deal of effort to do so. His mother can read and write, but a third of the women

[11] The first year of Peruvian elementary school is called *transición* and is not numbered.

her age cannot. Now, with more schools in the rural areas and busses to bring the children from outlying villages, only a seventh of the young women are illiterate. A generation ago few families bothered to make the effort necessary to educate a girl; consequently, more girls than boys were illiterate. Since the trouble of getting an education has been lessened, the number of literate boys and girls is about equal. Pedro is proud of his own education and says that it has contributed to his standing in the community. He regrets that he did not have enough to fit him for a technical occupation and points out that a poor man can only escape manual labor and continued poverty through education and technical skill.

Even though Pedro has to do much of his own cooking, the food in his house is standard for the village. When he gets up at six, Pedro usually has a cup of "tea" (not English tea, but some local herb) or instant coffee, a roll or two, a bit of cheese and olives, or perhaps a glass of soured milk. Pedro says that when he was a boy there was no bread in the village, but that the peasants ate *cancha*, maize kernels roasted in a pot of hot sand. Bread, as well as rice, has replaced the maize gruels and flour previously used in *tamales*. Even now, loaf bread is common only in the city; rolls are consumed in the rural area. *Tamales* were a common item of diet among the peasants in the last generation but are now eaten only on special festive occasions such as the processions at Yauca and Luren. Lunch is a hearty meal of soup, *seco* (rice, and perhaps bean paste, topped with meat scraps or an egg), and a side dish of maize. It is seldom highly spiced; such foods as *cebiche* (raw fish in lemon juice), *escabeche* (pickled fish or poultry), and *arroz con pato* (duck and rice) are eaten by the poorer classes only on festive occasions. Supper is usually made up of leftovers, a bit of bread, and tea. Pedro has a few grapevines left after tearing many out to plant cotton, and he still makes some wine and *pisco* in an old *falca* beside the house. He is fond of the young wine (*cachina*) as well as the fortified and likes his *pisco* with a bit of vermouth in it. Pedro and his friends were delighted when I showed them how to mix a boilermaker with *pisco* and beer, and they took to the drink like ducks to water. They no longer drink the traditional Peruvian *chicha* (maize beer) but prefer the bottled beer from Lima. *Chicha*, like *tamales* and some other foods, is now consumed only on special festive occasions.[12]

All Pedro's social activities center in San Juan and the surrounding countryside. He is a respected man in the community, having served several terms as *alcalde*, and occupies a social position among the villagers second to none. He does not visit the homes of his friends often — that is for women — but meets his cronies in the *cantinas* scattered through the village. When he goes to Ica and meets a friend there, they go to one of the little cafés on the Calle Grau, near the market, but never to the Trocadero, the Colón, or Navarro's. Pedro is one of the founders of the local sports club, which came into being about 1940, and is active in its affairs. He advises and directs the younger members and goes to the local soccer game every weekend.

Pedro is a religious man, but in a peculiarly peasant way. He goes to mass but often does not kneel at the proper time, largely out of a sense of independence and not because he is ignorant of the procedure. Even at the midnight Christmas mass (*misa de gallo*) he stood throughout the service with a haughty air. Like many men, he thinks that religion is more a matter for women. He attends the religious processions in Ica and Yauca, but more to see his cronies and have a good time than to participate in the religious aspect of the fiesta. Pedro thinks the priest in the village is an abominable person, but only a few of the peasants would agree with him. Many of them do not like the priest, but they hesitate to criticize him openly. Although he ignores some of the rituals of the church, Pedro is firmly convinced of the reality of some other supernatural phenomena. He says that he was once almost seized by a sand hill which suddenly came to life on a dark night, and that once the gate to the cemetery unlocked itself and banged back and forth in the wind. Once he had a cow that sickened and died of the evil eye. Pedro is well versed in the hot and

[12] On drinking patterns see Simmons 1959, 1960; Mangin 1957.

cold food taboos which are common in the valley but knows few home remedies, saying that these are matters for women. If he is sick, he usually goes to a doctor in Ica or takes patent medicines on the advice of a druggist.

Pedro has several *compadres* in the village and nearby areas. Most of those who solicited the favor of him are his social equals or perhaps slightly inferior to him in rank. The godfathers of his own children are a fairly wealthy peasant who lives outside the village and a small merchant in the city. Their rank is slightly higher than Pedro's, but the difference is small. Pedro has no *padrino* of marriage, since he was never married. Even those peasants who can afford to get married in church are often unable to find a *padrino*, because the expenses connected with the post are very heavy. They often select the Virgin and St. Anthony as their *padrinos*. Pedro cannot remember who his godfather was at baptism; that circumstance is not unusual, for godparent and godchild have no particularly close relationship. The relationship between the parent and godparent is the important one.

While Pedro is highly respected and liked by many of the villagers, he has some bitter enemies among them. He is the leader of one of the principal village factions, in which his closest associates are an accountant of a nearby hacienda, a tailor, and the secretary of the town council, who is his female cousin. Pedro gave her the job when he was *alcalde*, and his successor has been unable to oust her. It is said by his opponents that Pedro and his cousin, who live in adjoining houses, are really common-law spouses. I was once treated to a remarkable conversation between Pedro and his bitterest rival, in which the rival referred to the woman as "*tu mujer*" (your woman) and Pedro referred to her as "*mi prima*" (my cousin), each man pretending that he did not know what the other was talking about. Pedro's chief enemies are a schoolteacher and a mason; the latter is the godfather of a nephew whom Pedro raised from birth, and Pedro addresses the mason as "*compadre*." Contrary to the ideal pattern of respect in *compadrazgo*, the two are bitter enemies, although they address each other in the proper terms and refrain from outright conflict.[13]

[13] See Sayers 1956 on negative affect in *compadrazgo*.

Pedro has no *compadres* or close associates among the *hacendados* of the area, although he does most of his business with one of them. His land is surrounded on three sides by the property of another, and Pedro does not trust the man's intentions. He does not like to buy water from him, because the *hacendado* would be in a good position to take over his land if he could not pay.[14] Pedro admires the doctors and engineers of the public health service with whom he came in contact as *alcalde* and wishes that the government would do more in the way of free medical services for the peasants. The health service officials, on the other hand, think that Pedro is an ignorant man who understands little of modern medicine and sanitation, but who wants these services free. Said one doctor, "He thinks that the government owes him a living." They regard Pedro as he regards the landless laborers in the village — poor, ignorant, and grasping.

VI

Marcos Soria has a slightly lower formal position in the village than Pedro Romero but still falls within the lower middle class. He farms the family inheritance of six hectares jointly with his married brother and unmarried sister to avoid splitting up the property.[15] Almost all of the land is now in cotton, although there are some vines in the large garden in back of the house which he rents. He owns another, smaller house in the village but prefers to let it to another person and rent the more spacious one in which he lives.

Marcos' house is a typical one for a well-to-do peasant. It is of adobe, has concrete floors in the front room and bedrooms, a dirt floor in the kitchen, and a corral to the rear for storage and the chickens. The front half of the house contains the main room, flanked on either side by a bedroom which is reached through a curtain-hung doorway; the rear half of the house holds the large

14 About five years ago he was unable to buy water from the *hacendado* during a drought. Pedro's crop failed, and he had to sell three hectares to the *hacendado* to cover a bank loan; now he has only six hectares left.

15 Part of the six hectares is their inheritance, and part is adjoining land which Marcos bought from his father's brother, who, as Marcos put it, "is too lazy to farm and just wants a little cash to spend."

kitchen and a small storeroom. There is very little furniture. Each bedroom has a steel-frame bed, one of which is occupied by Marcos and his wife, the other by their two young daughters. A hammock cradle of crude sacking for their infant son hangs near the parents' bed. The front room contains a large, rough table covered with a dirty white cloth, as well as two chairs, several wall calendars and photographs, and the ubiquitous silver plaque of the Last Supper. In the kitchen are another table, some crude shelves, a chair, an adobe woodburning stove, the kerosene stove that replaced it, and a Primus kerosene burner. The house has electric lights when the town generator is in operation.

Marcos' younger brother, Pablo, lives about a block away in his own house. It is smaller than Marcos' but cleaner and more modern. All the floors are of concrete except in the *corral*, which is a small back room where the chickens run. Pablo's wife is a quiet, well-educated girl, admired by most of the village women for her knowledge and soft-spoken ways, and she likes "nice things" in her home. The dining room table is varnished and covered with a clean cloth. The new furniture in the front room is a type very common in lower-middle-class homes in the city and country — a copy of the Empire style, with varnished mahogany or blond woodwork and red or purple upholstered seats, often brocaded or embroidered in a floral pattern. One small table holds a vase of paper flowers; another has a radio. On the walls are photographs of the family, a picture of the Last Supper, and a small APRA banner (*Alianza Popular Revolucionaria Americana*), for Pablo is an ardent politician and embraces the party which is most popular among the lower classes.[16] Pablo's family are clearly "lace curtain" *cholos*.

Marcos and Pablo dress in khaki trousers and shirts in the village and usually remove their shoes to work in the fields. If they go to the city, they put on clean trousers and a white shirt. The women in the family dress just as the others of the village do. If they go

[16] One of the reasons for the greater luxury in Pablo's house is that he willingly accedes to his wife's demands and is proud of her elegant taste. Marcos has no patience with luxuries. As he put it, "For me it is enough to have good land and a big meal at noon; those who spend money for luxury or prefer money to land are fools."

to the city to shop, they put on clean cotton dresses, but if the occasion is a festive one, many of them imitate the kind of dress fashionable among the middle classes of Lima, of which the Gutiérrez and Vasco women furnish good examples.

Both Marcos and Pablo have finished primary school. Pablo's wife has had an equivalent amount of schooling, but Marcos' wife has only been as far as the third grade. All their education was in public schools. Most of the family have lived all their lives in the village; the peasants tend to be village- or district-endogamous, as opposed to men of the upper middle and upper classes, who frequently marry women from Lima. Marcos is the only one who has travelled widely; he was a member of the presidential guard during his compulsory Army service (a duty which Pablo managed to avoid) and has seen most of the country.

None of the Sorias or other villagers have any interest in what we would call art or intellectual activity. They read no books, play no musical instruments, make no objects of art, and decorate none of their utilitarian objects in an artistic way. The women do not make pottery, weave, or even embroider. The closest thing to art in their lives lies in the neatness of Pablo's house or in the flower arrangements that his wife helps make in the church on feast days. Marcos and Pablo do not even tell many stories or jokes, except in an occasional crude, heavy-handed reference to sex or some other physiological function. Their behavior is in strong contrast with that of the Indians of the sierra, who weave intricate textiles, play musical instruments, and have a razor-sharp sense of humor, even though they are poorer and have less formal education than the coastal people. If such activities were ever characteristic of Ica, they have been replaced by the products of modern factories, the radio and phonograph, and the sports page of the daily newspaper. The decline in proverb-telling in Ica is a case in point. According to the Escobars,[17] who made a study of proverbs in Ica, older people knew many more proverbs than younger people, and the importance of proverbs as an educational and recreational device had declined sharply.

In the other aspects of their life the Sorias are similar to

17 Escobar and Escobar 1954.

Romero. They eat the same food, drink the same liquor, and play the same kind of soccer. Marcos, who is a rather stern man, is aloof from the sports club, but his brother is devoted to it and would climb from his deathbed to see Sunday's game. The Sorias do not fit precisely into either of the political factions in the village; they get along well with Romero, but Pablo Soria is on bad terms with the tailor who is one of Romero's chief supporters. Marcos is respected in the village for his businesslike attitude, but his aloofness and his close relationship with a nearby *hacendado* win him few close friends. He has been a village councilman several times and may be appointed *alcalde* some day. Pablo was just appointed to the council for the first time.

Marcos and Pablo have positions in their households superior to those of their wives, although the women frequently take them to task and have them do various chores. Marcos complains that whenever his wife is pregnant she makes him haul all the water from their well. Marcos eats alone in his front room, leaving his wife and children in the kitchen, but Pablo and his wife and sister eat together. Both men are very fond of their children and affectionate to them; Marcos is particularly attached to his infant son.

Most of the *compadres* of the Soria family are in and around the village, but Marcos' *padrino* of marriage is a nearby *hacendado*. Marcos used to work for him as an errand boy before he went into the Army, and he was a trusted employee, reporting to the *hacendado* on the efficiency and honesty of the field hands. Now, if he needs well water quickly, or loan of a mule, a tractor, or money, the *hacendado* gives it to him. Understandably, some of the villagers are resentful of Marcos' close tie with his powerful neighbor and distrust him because of his earlier activities as a talebearer.

Like Romero, the Sorias are contemptuous of the poorer people in San Juan. Pablo, for example, points out that the poor seldom go to physicians when sick but consult the old women around the village and use a variety of herbal remedies. Some of them may even go to *curanderos*, he says. He himself uses medicines from the drugstore, a few herbal remedies, and goes to a doctor in serious cases. His wife prefers a trained and licensed midwife to the other practitioners of the trade, most of whom are old women of the area. Nevertheless, Marcos' wife takes their child to a *rezador* when it is sick, so that the *rezador* will make the sign of the cross and pray over it to drive out the illness. When the little girl has a fright and is afflicted with *susto*, Pablo employs a *llamador* to perform the complex ritual that will restore the girl to health.[18] Pablo says that most illnesses are caused by germs, which live in filth, but that there are some ailments that are not caused by germs and which are impervious to treatment by ordinary medical methods. *Susto* is certainly such an illness, as is the evil eye which so often strikes small children and against which the *rezador* is particularly effective.

VII

Members of the lower middle class in the city lead a somewhat different life from that of the peasants, and their social position is in some ways higher. An example of a man whose position is at the upper fringe of the lower middle class is Juan Tipacti, who lives in the village of Comatrana, just outside the city of Ica. Juan operates an express agency in the city and commutes between home and work by *colectivo*. His house is a spacious one; the front part is like that of Marcos Soria but is furnished in a more modern fashion, like Pablo's, and even has a new electric refrigerator. In back of the main section of the house is a row of small adobe rooms which are inhabited by Juan's grown sons and their families. His house is unusual in this respect: while many fathers allow their sons to remain in the house after marriage, Juan's often contains as many as thirty persons, including children. All the nuclear families have their own sleeping quarters but share the kitchen and other facilities.

At home, the men wear cotton trousers and shirts, particularly if they are engaged in any household chores, such as putting up a new adobe wall. In the city, their dress is more formal, consisting

[18] See particularly Rubel 1964 on the *susto* syndrome. For discussion of Peruvian folk medicine see Basto Girón 1957; Gillin 1947a; Montalvo 1967; Simmons 1955a; Valdizán and Maldonado 1922. For comparative data see Brown 1963; Clark 1959; Foster 1953a, 1967:184–193; Hudson 1951; Kelly 1956, 1965; Madsen 1961, 1964: ch. 8–11; Martínez and Martin 1966; Romano 1965; Rubel 1960; Saunders 1954; Simmons 1955a; Wellin MS, 1953, 1955.

of wool trousers, starched white shirts, and often coat and tie. The eldest Tipacti usually goes without a tie, but his sons, some of whom work in offices or government bureaus, normally wear them. The boys are careful to wear their neatest clothes in public and will not go into the city unless properly dressed. The women wear the same kind of clothes as those of the Soria household, and in matters of diet and drink the Tipactis are much like the Sorias and the Romeros.

Juan and his sons are extraordinarily well-educated. Juan has had a secondary school education and is fond of reading; one of his hobbies is learning foreign languages, and he speaks some English, Quechua, and Chinese in addition to Spanish. His eldest son, Carlos, who is a sanitary inspector, was educated on a scholarship at the University of Miami and speaks excellent English. He paints in oils as a hobby. Carlos has just obtained a job as sanitary inspector for an inter-American health program in the Caribbean. Another son, Pepe, has had only a Peruvian public school education like his father, but speaks fair English. The women of the family are also well-educated; Juan's wife conducts a small private elementary school in her home for the children of some neighbors. In addition, she gives sewing classes to a number of older girls. Carlos' wife is an intelligent and urbane woman; Pepe's is a peasant girl of lower-class family but clever within the limitations of her experience.

The social activities of the Tipacti family center in Comatrana and Ica. If the men meet friends in the city, it is usually at one of the small restaurants on the Calle Grau. The women visit neighbors in Comatrana frequently. Juan belongs to the Unión Social, and his membership illustrates his intermediate position between the lower middle and upper middle classes. Some of his *compadres*, godfathers of his sons, are members of the upper middle class and were old school chums of his. Juan remarks that *compadrazgo* among persons of his social position is not as formal a relationship as it is for those of lower status, particularly when compared to the *compadrazgo* of rural areas. He calls his *compadres* by the familiar form "*tu*," instead of using the traditional "*Usted*." One of Pepe's *compadres* is an executive in the government bureau where he works, and he addresses him as "*Usted*."

The Tipacti household is an affectionate one, and the members are loyal to one another, although there is some rivalry between Carlos and Pepe, who considers himself just as capable as but less fortunate than his elder brother. The boys admire their father for his high social standing and bookish interests. The women in the house are respected, but have a definitely inferior position. Pepe, in particular, is somewhat authoritarian in his relationships with his wife and eats apart from her. All of the Tipacti males were legally united with their spouses, although not all of them were married in church.

While the Tipacti womenfolk, like most of their sex, are more devout than the men, Juan and his sons are good Catholics. They go to mass and confession regularly, attend the major religious festivals, and contribute to the expenses of soliciting *mayordomías*. They do not, however, observe some of the smaller acts of faith, such as crossing themselves whenever they pass a church or roadside cross. In medical matters, Juan's education leads him to rely on professional physicians and modern medicines, and his sons, some of whom are employed by the health service, follow him in this. Nevertheless, Pepe's wife takes their daughter to a *rezador* when she cries for no apparent reason, and Pepe, himself a sanitary inspector, has employed a *llamador* when the child appeared to be stricken with *susto*. The women in the family use some home remedies, most of which are obtained at the drugstore, but some of which they buy from the herb sellers in the market or gather in the countryside. All the Tipactis are aware of the difference between hot and cold foods. They often observe the taboos connected with that classification but seldom phrase them in terms of hot and cold; they simply point out that eating pork and drinking cold water or drinking alcoholic beverages and eating mangoes will lead to a stomachache.

Juan and his sons regard themselves as part of the general population of Ica, but better educated and more fortunate than many. They are aware of their social superiority over most Iquenians, but do not regard the peasants as a separate race of beings, as Vasco or Gutiérrez would. On the other hand, Juan sees little real difference between his family and those of socially superior men, pointing with pride to the achievements of his eldest son.

The Tipactis are by no means a typical lower-middle-class family of Ica; they illustrate, instead, a family which is climbing into upper-middle-class status, "from the ranks" rather than from the provincial gentry. When Carlos Tipacti comes back from his scheduled five years in the Caribbean, he will be a relatively wealthy man, for the pay is good and he is a thrifty fellow. His education will be improved, his experience widened, and, in terms of local prestige, he will be as good a man as Jorge Vasco. One can see the beginnings of a middle middle class in Ica, and it will probably crystallize around people like Juan, Carlos, and Pepe Tipacti.

THE LOWER CLASS

VIII

One of Pepe Tipacti's close friends and colleagues is an employee of the sanitation service named Andrés Mosayguate. Because of his own urban residence, a secondary school education, and clerical position, Andrés is a member of the lower middle class, but he is at the lower fringe of it. His family is of typical lower-class peasant status. The combined inheritances of his father and mother comprise about a hectare of land, planted to cotton, grapes, and food crops.

Andrés' family lives in a small village in the center of the valley. The house stands close to others in the village and is attached to that of Andrés' paternal uncle, who is the father of Pepe Tipacti's wife. The home is built of *quincha*, or cane plastered with mud, and was erected by Andrés' father and uncle. It is about six or eight meters square, with a few glassless windows, a dirt floor, a door made of sawn planks, and an adjoining *corral*. The main room occupies the front half of the house and is furnished with a large table, a few straight chairs of willow wood with reed seats, a small table with a battery operated radio, and an imposing display of twenty-seven picture calendars. On one wall hangs a cracked mirror and a bobbed horsetail in which a communal comb is kept. The rear half of the house is divided into two sections, a bedroom and a kitchen. The bedroom is occupied by Andrés' parents, their eldest son, and his common-law wife and children. The kitchen doubles as a bedroom for the youngest son (about 18) and Andrés when he visits. The cooking facilities are separated from the beds in the kitchen by a cane frame covered with glued newspapers to make a screen. Cooking is done on a kerosene stove, although Sra. Mosayguate uses dried cotton stalks in an old wood-burning adobe stove when they are available.

Andrés' father dresses in dirty cotton trousers and a torn shirt and seldom wears shoes. Fifty years ago he would have worn knee breeches and a poncho, like a modern highlander. Andrés and his younger brother have a few pairs of good trousers and one good suit each, which they wear in the city or on formal occasions. Andrés typically wears gabardine trousers, a white shirt, a pull-over sweater, shoes, and socks in the city. The mother wears her hair in braids, dresses in a black cotton dress of simple cut, and often goes barefoot around the house. Her mother used to dress as a modern highland woman would now. The young children are usually dirty, attired in simple cotton dresses or short trousers and shirts, although boys under five usually have only the shirt and infants commonly are naked.

Of course, the family has no car but rides the country bus or a *colectivo* to travel to the city. Most travelling around the countryside is done on foot or with their donkey.

The elder Mosayguates are literate, but their education does not extend much beyond the ability to read, write, and do simple arithmetic. One of Andrés' uncles cannot read at all. Andrés, on the other hand, has had a public secondary school education and can read, write, and calculate with facility. Although he is not as intelligent as his friend Pepe and less strongly motivated, he has a reasonably firm basis for further education. He applied for admission to a university once but failed the entrance examinations. The younger brother has also finished secondary school but is less capable than Andrés. The elder brother has only a primary school education and is a factory laborer in the city.

Food at the Mosayguate table is like that of the other peasant families discussed. Soups, rice, sweet potatoes, lima beans, and *cancates* (a poor family's green peas) are the basis of the noon meal, with scraps of meat or an egg when they are to be had. The family eats very little fish. The kinds of fish which are highly regarded, such as corvina, are almost as expensive as meat, and most country people are ashamed to eat the cheaper varieties, such as bonito. Fish is also considered to be of low nutritional value and rather dangerous because of its very "cold" nature in the scheme of hot and cold classification of foods. Like the lower-middle-class peasants described above, the elder Mosayguate likes his wine and *pisco*. Andrés drinks wine but finds *pisco* a little strong; it is traditionally an old man's drink.

The males in the Mosayguate house eat at the table in the main room, and the women and children eat in the kitchen, often after the men have finished. The women have an inferior position in the household, although they argue vociferously with their husbands when the occasion demands it. The sons treat their mother with deference and respect, although they are sometimes embarrassed at her insistence that they "put on a sweater" or "comb their hair." Children are left to run as they please and are rarely disciplined until the parents think that they are old enough to understand.

The Mosayguates are a devout family. They go to church regularly and attend all the major religious festivals. Their village is one which has a principal role in the procession at Yauca, and Sra. Mosayguate assists in the preparation of the image of the village saint for the occasion, giving flowers from her garden and contributing money to the soliciting *mayordomo*. Her cousin, who lives in a nearby town, is the *mayorala* in charge of one of the masses at Yauca and has held that position for several years. The post is one of considerable prestige and demands great expenditures of energy and money. The success of a *mayordomo* or *mayorala* is measured by the opulence of the fiesta of which he is in charge, and he is heavily dependent on the other members of the *mayordomía* and on his friends for financial support. Thus, a successful fiesta is an indication of the personal influence and prestige of the *mayordomo*.

Sra. Mosayguate is well versed in herbal remedies and believes strongly in the efficacy of religious cures. She carefully passes a bit of cotton or a special herb over the image of the Virgin during the Yauca festival or over the statues in the Luren processions, and preserves the items as magical cures in case a stubborn illness should strike in the family. She says many of her sons' early illnesses were cured by prayer to the Virgin, by the ministrations of a *rezador* or *llamador*, or by the efficacy of religious tokens hung about the children's necks. Her husband's father was once bewitched by a *brujo* and eventually died, in spite of the family's employment of a noted *curandera* in Ica.

The social life of the Mosayguate family centers in their village. Sra. Mosayguate is active in the church and visits frequently with her neighbors. Sr. Mosayguate is a taciturn man, but often joins his friends for a drink in the *cantina*. One of Andrés' uncles is politically active and once participated in a peasant uprising in another village in which the prefect of the Department was killed (the Parcona uprising, 1923–1924). The Mosayguates have their closest relationships with their *compadres*. The sons' godparents are the lower-middle-class owners of a grocery store, and the elder Mosayguates have many godchildren among their neighbors. Andrés, too, is godfather to some of the small children in the village. *Compadres* in the village are seldom relatives and observe most of the traditional rules governing the relationship. They have no legal and hardly any moral obligation to their godchildren but are supposed to observe a strict respectful relationship with their *compadres*. They address each other as *"compadre"* and *"comadre"* and use the formal pronoun *"Usted"* even though they have been close friends from childhood.

While his parents' activities are traditional and center on church fiestas and obligations, Andrés is more active in the local soccer and social club. He is its president and also serves as an officer of the local cultural committee, which concerns itself with problems of building a village clubhouse and organizing the recreational aspect of religious fiestas. In these activities he is typical of most young peasants, who have abandoned the old religious organizations and seek personal influence and prestige through the medium of amateur soccer. The soccer clubs have taken over many of the social functions of the *mayordomías* in serving as a local rallying point and providing a means of wealth display in their team uniforms and fiestas. The inter-village rivalry carried on in the soccer games has replaced the old organized gang fights which used to occur between the young men of different villages, and soccer, as a sport, has almost totally displaced cockfighting. Andrés never goes to cockfights, although his father occasionally does, and only his grandfather had frequent opportunities to see bullfights in the valley.

Andrés' attitudes toward the other social classes in Ica are complicated by his intermediate position between the lower class and the lower middle class. He is loyal to his parents, particularly to his mother, but vaguely ashamed of their "backward" ways. He helps his father in the farm work at peak seasons but finds this manual labor hard to reconcile with the white-collar job he has in the city. (Andrés still has the typical peasant reflex of kicking off his shoes before walking into a plowed field.) He would rather think himself an equal of the Tipactis than a typical rural peasant, and he seeks to be a true *criollo*. As he defines it, a true *criollo* is a man who has a pleasant and easy manner, makes clever jokes, is in complete command of himself, has a good job which requires small effort but yields good pay, and is a dapper ladies' man. Andrés is too conscious of his rural lower-class background to be a real *criollo*. He tries to be gay with the ladies but only succeeds with the ones from his home village; he is much too shy to approach a strange woman.

On the other hand, some of his urban acquaintances are the acme of *criollismo*. Among the best *criollos* Andrés knows are two guitar players (one of whom is Ica's chief ratcatcher) who are in frequent demand at the fiestas in the city. They play excellently, concentrating on the modern *vals criollo* style although they can perform the *marinera* as well; neither one of them can play a *huayno*. Sometimes they have fiestas of their own, where three or four guitars are going at once, one friend plays a trumpet, another a clarinet, and a third the bongo drums. They dress immaculately but often without ties, and their shoes shine like mirrors. Their conversation is rapid, clever, and full of sexual allusions. When they meet an attractive woman on the street, they frequently stop and stare at her dramatically, or follow her for a short distance, complimenting her on her appearance: *"Mi alma, mi corazón, reina morena de mi vida . . ."* ("My soul, my heart, dark queen of my life . . ."). If the woman, too, is *criolla*, she merely smiles and walks on, perhaps undulating a little more under her skin-tight dress. Andrés can hardly manage a smile at a pretty girl and is embarrassed by discussions of the beauty of women on the street. If his sisters are complimented by a strange man, they simply giggle furiously.

The *criollo* pattern is thus of limited distribution in the society, characteristic of the lower fringe of the upper class and of the urban middle and lower classes but aspired to by the rural middle and lower classes. Even the highlanders on the coast speak of their social aspirations in terms of becoming *criollo*. In its present form, *criollismo* is a historical combination of upper-class and lower-class behavior and varies from class to class. Its most devoted practitioners are the urbanites of Lima, and the capital is regarded in the provinces not so much as the national center of political power but as the fountainhead of modern Peruvian culture.[19]

The Mosayguate family is not at the bottom of the Iquenian lower class by any means. There are many local peasants, such as the standing-renters in Ocucaje, who are much poorer than they, but the differences between them are matters of degree rather than of kind. The poorest families live in huts of cane which are sometimes even devoid of mud plaster. They eat almost no meat, eggs, or fish, and dress in the most ragged of clothes, although their clothes are of coastal rather than of highland type (i.e., shirts and trousers rather than breeches and ponchos). They are more inclined to practice folk medicine and participate in the local religious fiestas, although they rarely can afford to assume the position of *mayordomo*. Like most peasants, they play soccer, but their conservatism is shown in their continuing addiction to cockfights.

THE LOWER LOWER CLASS

Beneath these people in the social scale are the recent migrants from the sierra. I was unable to make friends with any of them, because of their deep distrust of any white man, and cannot describe their lives and attitudes in detail.[20] As we have noted pre-

[19] Simmons 1955b.

[20] Their attitudes toward whites are like those of many Negroes in the United States and stem from the same history of servile exploitation and paternalism (see Rowe 1957). In 1957–1958 they were morbidly afraid of a mythical scourge, the *pistacos*, two *gringos* who drove about in a red pickup truck kidnapping fat Indians to melt them down for grease. The immediate cause of this phenomenon was said to lie in rumors begun by Bolivian Com-

viously, the *serranos* dress more conservatively than the local peasants. The women wear colorful blouses and full skirts and have their hair in long braids, often with colored thread twined into the hair. The men usually wear ordinary trousers (as do many Indians even in the sierra), but I have seen them with ponchos. Most of these articles of dress are probably of colonial Spanish derivation. The inevitable mark of a *serrano* in Ica is a crumpled felt hat, often worn by women as well as men. The coastal peasants wear straw hats, and felt ones reappear on the coast only among members of the upper class when they are formally dressed. Many *serranos* speak no Spanish, and those who do have a marked accent.

In general, the *serranos* are miserably poor. When they first come to Ica they usually do so as migrant agricultural laborers, returning to their own mountain plots for planting and harvest. Some of them stay on as permanent laborers on the great haciendas of the valley; some also take work as porters or restaurant waiters in the city, and the women enter into petty shopkeeping. The permanent fruit and vegetable stalls in the market are almost all operated by *serranas*. The great desire of the highlanders is to become *criollo*, which they understand to be a person who enjoys a secure standard of living, does relatively little menial work, plays soccer, goes to the cinema, speaks Spanish fluently, and is confident and poised in social situations. Some of them achieve

---

munists, who accused the United States of evil deception in its shipment of wheat to the southern highlands after a severe drought, saying that the purpose was to fatten Indians, since an injection of human fat was necessary to start jet airplane engines. There is historical precedent for the myth; in colonial and early republican times, it was said that the sugar mills could not commence annual operations until the machinery had been greased with human fat, and major Inca building projects were often commenced with the burial of human sacrifices. The situation was tense in 1957 when two *gringo* prospectors in the southern highlands (who were unfortunately driving a pickup truck) were surrounded by highlanders and seriously beaten; the owner of an upvalley hacienda declined to lend me a mule to explore the upper canyon of the Ica on the grounds that I would probably not come back.

For descriptions of Indian life in the Andean highlands, see Argüedas 1964; Bouruncle Carreón 1964; Castillo 1964a, 1964b, 1964c, 1964d; Collier and Buitrón 1949; Escobar 1964; Fried 1962; Holmberg 1960; Mangin 1957, 1960, 1964a, 1964b, 1965, 1967; Martinez 1963; Matos 1964; Mishkin 1964; Nuñez del Prado 1955, 1964; Parsons 1945; Price 1965; Stein 1961; Vásquez 1965; Vásquez and Holmberg 1966. Tumin 1952 provides comparative data on Indian-mestizo relations in Guatemala.

Representatives of the lower classes: top left, *a young man on the way up, a social equal of Andrés Mosayguate of the lower class;* top right, *a highland girl of the lower lower class with thorns in one hand and barbed wire in the other;* bottom, *highlanders seated in the courtyard of the church in Luren, next to a candle seller's stand.*

105

these goals for themselves, particularly if they come to the coast as young adults and remain there for fifteen or twenty years. After that length of time they are usually accepted by their neighbors, although one can still hear an occasional murmur of *"serrano"* behind their backs. For their children, it is another matter. Regardless of their parentage, if they are born or brought up in Ica and absorb the local lower-class ethos from an early age, there is no question as to their status; they are *criollos*, at least from a highlander's point of view.

SUMMARY

The principal gaps in the general social scale lie between the upper middle and lower middle classes and between the lower and lower lower classes.[21] Most individual political and economic power is held by members of the upper and upper middle classes. Members of the lower middle and sometimes of the lower class may have political and economic power in their labor unions or political organizations, but their effect as individuals is limited to action within these and other minor organizations such as soccer clubs. The lower lower class has no effective political or economic influence except as a source of cheap labor.

Although the general, oligarchic pattern of the republican period is still evident in the modern social scale there have been some striking changes. Chief among these is the extent to which the lower and lower middle classes are now copying the behavior transmitted to them by mass communications media. The old pattern of imitation within the hierarchy of the valley, modified as it may have been by some inter-class contact between areas, has been augmented by extensive borrowing from the upper-class and upper-middle-class sources of Euro-American culture provided by the cinema and from the lower-class and lower-middle-class sources of urban Lima which are in more intense contact with the provinces than ever before. The pattern of intra-societal diffusion has been sufficiently modified so that members of the lower classes adopt behavior that their local superiors have never practiced and of which they may strongly disapprove.

---

[21] In local terms, the three major segments of society are labelled *blanco*, *cholo*, and *indio*.

CHAPTER EIGHT

*An
Overview*

The changes in Iquenian society and culture over the past four hundred years have been extensive and complex.[1] The very face of the land has been altered, and the valley peopled by new racial and ethnic groups. In the period for which we have adequate information, the economic system has passed through successive phases of plantation agriculture and expanding commercial development, and it now finds itself in a period of rapidly increasing industrialization and technological specialization. New artifacts and modes of behavior have eliminated almost all traces of the pre-Columbian past, and little remains even of the colonial heritage. These changes in the content of the Iquenian scene have been presented in the text in such a way that some of the direct relationships between them are obvious. For example, many of the

[1] For comparable discussions on other areas see Faron 1960; Gillin 1960; Holmberg, Dobyns, and Vásquez 1961.

recent changes in agricultural techniques came about as the result of the basic adoption of well irrigation.

Other aspects of the process, however, are not as self-evident; these concern the nature of the social substructures of wealth, authority, and prestige. What were these substructures like at various times in Iquenian history? How have they changed, and what have been the interrelationships among them?

Of the three substructures, the simplest to investigate is that of political authority. The most striking changes in it are those of the third type mentioned in the Introduction, in which the "shape" of the substructure, the relative positions of its components, has altered. Under the Inca Empire, authority stemmed directly from the head of state and was concentrated in a small class of nobles. The substructure was a unilineal one. In the early colonial period, authority was somewhat divided, and the system was bilineal, since the native *caciques* retained a degree of autonomy and power over the native Indian population. However, authority still derived ultimately from the apex of the political pyramid, then in Spanish hands. The complexity of the early colonial structure was eliminated by the abolition of special *cacique* powers, and the system reverted to an essentially unilineal one by the nineteenth century. The revolution against Spain removed the last traces of monarchic organization in a *coup d'état* and led to the *de jure* recognition of independent creole power that had been developing within the authority structure during colonial times. Until recently, the creole revolution was the only successful development of independent political influence at a subordinate point on the authority scale.

In the last two decades, however, organized and self-conscious foci of power have been developing at such subordinate points. Many of them are labor unions; others are political parties such as the Communist or APRA, which are popular with the lower and lower middle classes. For the first time, the balance of political power includes not only competing factions of high status (such as *caciques* against Spaniards or creoles against peninsulars in colonial times) but also groups whose humble position in the overall social scale is recognized even by themselves. The rise of proletarian groups to political eminence is in some ways a result of indigenous economic changes but was directly stimulated by extra-Peruvian developments. The active source of the change is the same intellectual and moral ferment that led to the Russian revolution and to social and labor reform measures in the rest of Europe and the United States, communicated to the Peruvian lower classes by European-oriented liberals such as González Prada, Mariátegui, and Haya de la Torre. I have touched only briefly on these matters in the text, for they are mainly urban developments, with their Peruvian focus in Lima, and are Iquenian only in their effects.

Another recent change of similar type is involved in the general centralization of political power in Lima and the decline of independent figures of local authority, as well as the increase in direct local influence of persons who divide their attentions between affairs in Lima and Ica. For example, the functions of regulating water rights and collecting most taxes have passed from the hands of locally influential provincials to the national bureaucracy. Further, the members of the upper class who formerly controlled political affairs in Ica through a chain of patronage from their residence in Lima now more frequently enter directly into the local political scene. These developments were possible only after the evolution of an efficient system of communication between Ica and Lima and result from the continuing efforts toward maximization of political power by the members of the national oligarchy. The increased control of that oligarchy is offset by the rise of corporate proletarian political groups, as noted above, which also take advantage of the efficient communication to exercise direct influence in national government without recourse to the old intermediate chain of patronage.[2]

The substructure of authority, then, has passed from the unilineal one of the Inca Empire, through the bilineality of the early colonial period, back to a unilineal type in the nineteenth century, and now finds itself in a multilineal condition. The process has been a fluctuation between simplicity and complexity, moved by the appearance of independent foci of political power at points

[2] See Patch 1966 for a discussion of recent political developments. For comparative material on Argentina see Germani 1965.

along the scale of authority. The complexity of the twentieth century, however, is different from that of the sixteenth, since the independent pressure groups which currently have direct access to the source of national authority are of a much lower overall social status than the *caciques* or creoles of the colonial period. Despite its more inclusive representative base, however, the system is still similar to those of former times in that authority continues to derive from the apex of the political pyramid. The democratic ideal espoused by the liberals noted above, in which the ultimate locus of authority is not the apex but the base of the pyramid, has not been achieved. It is scarcely necessary to observe that that ideal is seldom achieved in any complex society.

Other changes in the substructure can be specified only with difficulty. It is possible that the multilineality of the modern political system allows greater individual mobility within it, or at least more avenues for that mobility, than could have been found in the late colonial or republican systems. The historical data are inadequate to pursue the question further. On the other hand, it does seem as if a negative change of type two (see page 4) has occurred over time; in general, fewer aspects of human life are controlled by political figures, and the extent of authority exercised seems less than before.

The second substructure to be considered is that of wealth. While it has some tangible content and is thus easier to perceive, it is more complicated than the substructure of authority, since its material characteristics have varied through time. First, individual ownership of productive property was restricted or perhaps nonexistent in preconquest times; extensive private ownership of land and capital began with the Spanish conquest. Second, the aboriginal economic system was based on exchange or payment in kind; money was introduced by the Europeans. These European introductions diffused gradually through the society as a whole, and some features of the earlier systems persisted until recent times. The effects of the introductions, therefore, were not immediate and complete and must be considered step by step at various points on the historical continuum.

In the Inca Empire all land and major capital was theoretically in the hands of the state. The only kind of "wealth" that was differentially distributed through the society was control of labor, and its distribution led to a twofold division of the population: those who engaged in productive manual labor and those who controlled manual labor by engaging in executive, non-manual labor. As we will note later, the correspondence among degree of political authority, prestige, and wealth (in the sense of control over labor) was very high, so that none of the substructures can be finely divided without reference to the others.

In the colonial period state ownership of land and capital gave way to private ownership, culminating eventually in the effective disappearance of communal Indian lands. A money economy was introduced at the top of the overall social scale, and it penetrated downward to the level of smallholders with the adoption of grape cultivation. Direct labor control, without the intervention of cash, continued in the utilization of slaves, any sharecroppers who may have existed, and Indian corvée labor.

After the slaves and bondservants were freed in the republican era, direct labor control continued in sharecropping but was combined with concurrent wage labor in the vineyards. Cash payment for services thus became more extensive among the lower classes. After cotton was subsumed under the sharecropping system for field crops, the production of goods for cash exchange, as well as wage labor, became more common among landless laborers. When the sharecropping system was abandoned, cash payment for labor as well as for the products of individual agricultural activity became the rule in the entire society. The intensification of the cash economy is correlated as well with the disappearance of cooperative peasant labor and of corvée labor on irrigation works in exchange for special water rights. Erasmus' conclusion [3] that the increased use of cash tends to destroy the basis of cooperative peasant labor exchange is thus confirmed; the Ica data suggest, however, that the concept of cooperative labor should be expanded to include corvée labor and sharecropping as symbiotic or cooperative forms that also decline with the intensification of cash economy.

[3] Erasmus 1956, MS.

These changes in the *bases* of the substructure of wealth tend to obscure some of the other structural changes that have occurred. Nevertheless, two principal types of change are evident. First, there has been a change of the third type mentioned in the Introduction, in which the entire society has moved "up" the wealth scale, or, viewed conversely, in which the means or articles of wealth have moved down through the society. The general standard of living in Ica has risen, so that the society as a whole is "wealthier" than before. This change, in itself, does not constitute an alteration in the relative positions in the substructure of wealth; the poor, although richer, are still poor.

The second change, however, does represent an alteration in relative position and is a change of the second type previously discussed. It concerns the increasing concentration of wealth in fewer and fewer hands, as outlined in the text. Part of this concentration has come about as a result of large investors and operators "squeezing out" smaller ones, as the former have expanded their activities. Part of the concentration has stemmed from a particular factor in capital expansion — the increase in specialization and technological improvements. Initially, the cost of specialization and technological improvements (as in installing a winery or equipping a deep well) was so high that only the wealthier operators could afford them. Once the innovations had been made, however, they provided a more efficient return than the older processes, so that the wealthier operators were able to realize even greater profits than before as soon as the initial investment in the technological improvements had been repaid. Thus, the more wealth an individual had, the more profitably it could be invested, and there arose a larger gap between small and large operators than that which had existed before. Wealthy modern operators can expand faster than small, traditional ones, and at the same time the increasingly high cost of technological improvements makes it more difficult for relatively poor operators to invest in those improvements that would give them the same technological advantages enjoyed by their wealthier fellows.

This spiralling, self-reinforcing change in the distribution of wealth appears to be only the initial phase of a longer process.

First, capitalization and technological improvement are now becoming so expensive even for wealthy operators that they often require a corporate base, in which relatively small investments can yield a return. The strong increase in corporate land ownership among the wealthy classes, and its appearance even in the lower middle class, is illustrative of the trend.[4] The informal and impermanent but sometimes recurrent associations of small farmers to rent tractors or purchase well water in combination provide further examples. If this trend continues, persons with relatively little capital may be able to achieve in concert what they could not do individually, and the present structural gap below the large operators may diminish.

Second, the requirements of technical and managerial skill in modern operations are becoming increasingly great, so that the real wages of skilled manual, clerical, and directive workers may be expected to rise. The relative wealth of these individuals, compared to that of unskilled laborers *and* capitalists, will therefore increase; the change has already begun to occur and should intensify as the increasingly technical farms and factories expand. This change, too, should contribute toward the diminution of the gap between very wealthy persons and the rest of the population, provided of course that the increasing concentration of wealth in the upper strata does not accelerate.

Summarizing, it seems that modernization of productive activities first created an economic situation in which small, traditional, independent operators were eliminated from competition and in which large operators assumed more extensive control of the means of production. Modernization, however, became necessary for the efficient maintenance of a competitive productive enterprise. The requirements of modernization are now such that they demand a corporate base for investment and further improvement and a skilled laboring and managerial class to operate the enterprises. If the process of industrialization continues in its

[4] The 1961 agro-economic census shows that 54 percent of the agricultural area in the Department in plots over five hectares is held by *sociedades mercantiles* (business firms), while almost no land in smaller plot sizes is so held. Ninety-three percent of the large owners (with more than five hectares) were business firms.

present course, we may expect further diminution of individual, entrepreneurial wealth and an increase in the relative wealth of the skilled technical and managerial class. The limit which these changes approach is an eventual closure of the gaps in the scale of wealth, so that, while differences in wealth will persist, they will be more uniformly graded through the society.

Again, changes in individual mobility are difficult to assess; while no statement can be made on the *rate* of mobility, it seems as if the possible *avenues* of mobility are greater in number than before. Just as in matters of authority, there seem to be more individual alternatives for advance or retrogression.[5]

The last of the substructures to be examined is that of prestige. As noted in the Introduction, the basis for establishment of a substructure of prestige is the determination of the nature of prestigeful behavior and its distribution in the society. How do we know what kinds of behavior carry prestige? In a contemporary situation, we have the stated value judgments of informants: "It is better to be literate than illiterate"; "Whiskey is better than *pisco*"; "A chinaware dish is better than a gourd one." It is only rarely that such explicit statements are available for the past, however, and we must rely on inferential establishment of what was prestigeful. We are assisted in this inference by the general rule that individuals in a culture tend to imitate prestigeful behavior. While not all prestigeful behavior is imitated, and while behavior lacking prestige is sometimes imitated, imitation is generally a *de facto* recognition by the imitator of the prestige of the individual or class from which the behavior was copied. Thus, the *route* of intrasocietal diffusion of behavior is a clue to the nature of the prestige scale.

Most intrasocietal diffusion follows the formal class structure of a society; innovations tend to be made or first accepted by the upper class and then diffuse downward through the rest of the society.[6] This is a kind of perpetual occurrence of a type three

[5] For recent theoretical discussion and empirical studies on mobility and economic development see Smelser and Lipset 1966; Hammel MS.

[6] Fallers 1954; Hammel 1964b; Rowe MS; Rowe *et al.* MS; Tarde 1895; Veblen 1953.

change in the substructure of prestige. Many features of upper-class behavior are directly dependent on the possession of wealth, such as automobiles, higher education, and the habit of drinking whiskey instead of *pisco*. These tend to diffuse slowly through the society, depending either on the prior acquisition of wealth by the imitators or on the cheapening of the item considered. Other items are not so restricted, such as habits of speech, music, or dress, and these tend to diffuse more rapidly. Similarly, certain items of behavior may be restricted to individuals holding a particular degree of political authority and are symbolic of authoritative positions; these, too, diffuse very slowly or not at all. The modes of dress included in the sumptuary laws of medieval Europe or the Inca Empire furnish good examples.[7] Despite the generally close correspondence between *some* kinds of prestigeful behavior and degree of wealth or authority, our inability to specify the nature of the correspondence at different times and places makes it advisable to consider the substructure of prestige separately from those of wealth and authority.

In the Inca Empire the kinds of behavior that symbolized prestige were rigidly fixed. As we will see below, they were intimately connected with the grades of the substructure of authority and doled out to subordinates by the head of state. As far as we know, there was no independent individual mobility in the prestige scale; all shifts were made in the authority scale, and prestige ranking followed as a concomitant.

In the colonial period, certain items of aboriginal behavior were immediately adopted by the Spaniards. Some local foods, such as

[7] If members of high status groups adopt or create particular patterns of behavior in an effort to differentiate themselves from lower status groups, the subsequent adoption of such behavior at a lower social level destroys the symbolic utility of that behavior for the higher status group. Thus, the effort made by the higher status group toward symbolic differentiation must be a continuing one. If the adoption of their behavioral patterns by lower status groups is restricted by economic or proscriptive factors, or by sheer impossibility of imitation (such as membership in a kin group), little innovation would be necessary. On the other hand, patterns of behavior that were not so limited would tend to diffuse rapidly and would, therefore, exhibit a higher rate of innovation in the upper strata of a society. The suggested phenomenon may be a factor in the greater degree of change shown in patterns of dress, diet, music, and other forms of entertainment.

the *lúcuma* or potato, although they had no apparent differential distribution within the native social structure, were "low-class," i.e., non-Spanish, in the colonial system. Nevertheless, they were adopted by the conquerors; even Spaniards had to eat. Some animals, such as the pack llama, or methods of agriculture, such as *poza* irrigation, were also indigenous and therefore "low-class," in the sense of direct usage as well as of indirect employment, in which lower-class workers used them for the benefit of upper-class overseers. The Spaniards adopted the managerial behavior of the native upper class in continuing these productive methods, even though the native upper class was below them in the colonial social scale. We may regard this kind of borrowing as expectable in contact or conquest situations; it is a form of maximization of economic opportunity, illustrating the relative values of "prestige" versus "wealth" and constituting a specific and definable exception to the general rule of downward diffusion.

Subsequently, borrowing seems to have been down the overall social scale. Habits of dress and diet, of music and the dance, diffused with relative ease, successively adopted and abandoned by the lower classes as the downward diffusion progressed. Innovation continued at the upper levels of the class system, so that there was a stream of new behavior passing through the society; some items which were characteristic of upper-class behavior in the colonial period passed through all the levels and have almost disappeared. A convenient example is the *tamal*, probably introduced by the Spaniards from Mexico. It eventually became a common item of lower-class diet but is now found only in traditional or ritual situations such as major religious festivals, where a conscious attempt is made to preserve older customs. Even there, it is limited to the lower classes. Thus, there was a certain amount of intrasocietal imitation going on in colonial times. However, many symbols of prestige, principally in matters relating to taxation and forced labor, were rigidly fixed in an intricate legal system based on ethnic origin. The rapidity with which any individual could adopt prestigeful behavior was therefore restricted by political as well as economic considerations; individual mobility along the prestige scale was low.

116

In republican times most of the restrictive features of the colonial legal system disappeared. Imitation was probably more frequent as the acculturation of the native Indian population, slaves, and bond servants progressed, and some features, such as the *marinera* dance, diffused very rapidly through the society. Originally introduced to Lima from France in the 1800's, the *marinera* was eventually adopted (after many artistic reinterpretations and changes) by the lower classes of Peruvian society, including those of Ica. In most of the coastal areas, like Ica, it has since lost popularity to more modern dances.

The distinctive feature of all these prestige scales — Inca, colonial, and republican — is that they were essentially unilineal. No change in the character of the substructure of prestige seems to have occurred until recently. Over the last three or four decades, however, the lower and lower middle classes in Ica have ceased to imitate only (or principally) the classes immediately above them in the valley and have begun to copy the examples of Euro-American culture provided by the cinema, radio, and newspapers. New behavior now enters the overall social scheme from two directions — from the top, as before, and broadside into the lower classes. In terms of the types of change discussed in the Introduction, this is a change of type three, in which the shape of the substructure has changed. First, it short-cuts the old path of acculturation, because the lower classes may copy directly the same models to which their local social superiors look for innovation. Second, the lower classes often adopt forms of behavior which their superiors in Ica reject.[8]

On an individual level these changes mean that prestige may be gained by additional means, that the number of alternatives for behavior is greater, and that individual mobility in the substructure of prestige is probably greater than before. On the level of national Peruvian society, it means that the independence and isolation of local class hierarchies is breaking down, and that separate localities are no longer connected only (or principally) by their respective elites. Members of the lower middle class, for

[8] Cf. Martínez 1965; Varallanos 1962; Wolf 1956.

example, are now subjected to many of the same cultural influences simultaneously in a number of locales in Peru without the intermediacy of the upper classes in their respective hierarchies. Further, members of that class (or of other subordinate classes) often communicate directly with each other over long distances. Modern communication has been instrumental in creating a national society out of a series of provincial ones.[9]

These have been the principal changes in the abstracted dimensions of Iquenian social structure. What can be said about the relationships between them and the coherence of the total social scheme at different points in time? What have been the changes of the fourth type suggested in the Introduction?

In Inca times the degree of fit between the three substructures was very close. In fact, it was so close that they scarcely had independent meaning. Private wealth in our sense was essentially nonexistent, and prestige and its symbols were directly proportional to the degree of administrative authority held. Insofar as freedom from manual labor constituted wealth (in the sense of command over resources), no man had wealth without a position of authority, or any degree of authority without its precise concomitant of symbolic prestige. The axis of this monolithic and totalitarian social structure seems to have been political authority. Individual mobility within the system could be achieved only by revolution or fiat; the first course seems to have been rare, but the second was not. The rapid expansion of the Empire offered frequent vacancies in the political structure, and individuals were often shifted within it. The monolithic character of the system, although it provided only a single avenue of mobility, thus did not dampen the rate of mobility; that was maintained by the exigencies of the expanding, imperialist society and by despotic whim.

In the colonial period most wealth passed into private hands. Political authority was vested directly in the state and flowed from it, but it tended to follow the lines of wealth distribution, so that wealthy men were often powerful because of their wealth and not only on the basis of legal sanction. However, authority was

[9] Cf. Lerner 1958.

still important in maintaining and acquiring wealth. Some features of the prestige system were distributed on a legal basis, and others tended to follow the lines of wealth; some, however, diffused more freely. As the untrammeled capitalism of colonial times expanded, the old relationships among wealth, authority, and prestige began to break up, reaching a major reorganization in the creole revolution. That reorganization was a recognition of the primacy of wealth as a criterion of social ranking and as a means of obtaining authority and prestige; the basic dimensions of the social structure became wealth instead of authority, although the new pattern was probably as tightly organized as the previous one, and the congruence between social substructures was still high.

The republican system continued until recently (ca. 1920), when marked changes in all three substructures led to a wider divergence among them. Wealth is still the major factor in social organization, since persons of wealth usually enjoy both prestige and authority commensurate with their riches. One can thus describe the modern social structure more elegantly in terms of wealth than in terms of either prestige or authority. However, authority may be had without individual wealth, as the rise of proletarian political groups and the new lines of political influence indicate, and prestige may be gained without following the lines of the local wealth structure, as indicated by the new sources of innovation among the lower classes. Since these separate structures are no longer necessarily congruent as they were in Inca or early colonial times, or as closely related as they were in the later colonial or republican periods, it follows that change along any one of the dimensions is more independent than before.

If we consider the cultural changes basic to these developments, it is clear that the increased fluidity of communication and economic transaction (via a cash economy) were largely, although not totally, responsible. The society of Ica today is an organic part of the national scene and has cultural contacts over a vastly extended area. While the increase in inter-area contact between equivalent classes has made the class structure more uniform and perhaps more rigid as a national classificatory system, it is evident that freedom of choice is greater, and that cultural alternatives and avenues of social mobility are more numerous than before. The data from Ica suggest as well that the recent multilineality within the substructures of wealth, authority, and prestige, as well as the divergence among them, may allow an increase in the *rate* as well as in the *avenues* of individual mobility in the overall social structure. Whether that increase has in fact occurred, and is a proposition applicable to other social systems, is a matter for further research.

If we were to summarize these changes in a few words, we would of course say that the society of Ica has become more complex and that its organic solidarity has increased. These phenomena, indeed, would be perceptible even in an ordinary survey of Iquenian history, but I have here described them more rigorously and, more importantly, in structural terms, free of the constraints imposed by a single culture, so that they may be applicable in the comparative study of social change.

Bibliography

Note: A somewhat fuller bibliography of items pertaining to the Ica Valley itself will be found in Hammel 1959, 1962a.

Adams, Richard N.
1953   "A Change from Caste to Class in a Peruvian Sierra Town." *Social Forces* 31:238–244.
1964   "Rural Labor." In John J. Johnson (Ed.), *Continuity and Change in Latin America*. Stanford: Stanford University Press, pp. 49–78.

Álvarez Andrews, Óscar
1951   "Las clases sociales en Chile." *Revista Mexicana de Sociología* 13:201–220. Universidad Nacional Autónoma, Instituto de Investigaciones Sociales, México.

Anicama, Pedro
MS.   *Razón de las tierras que poseían los indios del repartimiento de Hanan en términos y jurisdicción de la ciudad de Ica, hecha por don Pedro Anicama, cacique y gobernador de aquel repartimiento.* Archivo Nacional del Perú, Derecho Indígena, Legajo 9, Cuaderno 211, Año 1718, 11 lvs.

121

Anonymous
MS. *Discricion general del reyno de Piru em particular de Lima.*
Paris: Bibliothèque Nationale, Département de Manuscrits,
Espagnol 280 f 1–235, ca. 1605–1615.
Argüedas, José María
1964 "Puquio, una Cultura en Proceso de Cambio." In José María
Argüedas (Ed.), *Estudios Sobre la Cultura Actual del Perú.*
Lima: Universidad Mayor de San Marcos, pp. 221–272.
Basto Girón, Luís J.
1957 *Salud y Enfermedad en el Campesino Peruano del Siglo
XVII.* Lima: Universidad Nacional Mayor de San Marcos,
Facultad de Letras, Instituto de Etnología y Arqueología.
Beals, Ralph L.
1953 "Social Stratification in Latin America." *American Journal of
Sociology* 58:327–339.
Blanchard, W. O., and Elizabeth Blanchard
1929 "The Grape Industry of Spain and Portugal." *Economic Ge-
ography* 5:183–193.
Bouruncle Carreón, Alfonso
1964 "Contribución al Estudio de las Aymaras." (In two parts.)
América Indígena 24(2):129–169; 24(3):233–269.
Brown, Jack
1963 "Some Changes in Mexican Village Curing Practices Induced
by Western Medicine." *América Indígena* 23(2):93–120.
Calancha, Fr. Antonio de la
1639 *Coronica moralizada del Orden de San Avgvstin en el Perv,
con svcesos egenplares :vistos: en esta monarqvia.* Vol. 1,
Barcelona: P. Lacavalleria.
Carrera Vergara, Eudocio
1954 *La Lima criolla de 1900. Corregida y aumentada.* Lima.
Caso, Francisco, Ricardo Caso, and Pedro Caso
1950 *Tres hermanos.* Lima.
Castelnau, Francis de
1851 *Expédition dans les parties centrales de l'Amérique du Sud,
de Rio de Janeiro à Lima et de Lima au Parà; exécutée par
ordre du gouvernement français pendant les années 1843 à
1847 sous la direction de Francis de Castelnau. Histoire du
voyage.* Vol. 4, Paris: P. Bertrand.
Castillo, Hernán
1964a *Carcas: The Forgotten Community.* Ithaca: Cornell University Department of Anthropology, Cornell Peru Project.
1964b *Chaquicocha: Community in Progress.* Ithaca: Cornell University Department of Anthropology, Cornell Peru Project.
1964c *Accopata: The Reluctant Recipient of Technological Change.*
Ithaca: Cornell University Department of Anthropology, Cornell Peru Project.
1964d *Mito: The Orphan of its Illustrious Children.* Ithaca: Cor-

nell University Department of Anthropology, Cornell Peru
Project.
Castro Bulnes, J. Isaac
MS.   Letter to T. E. Letts, Inspector de la Zona Sur, Dirección de
Aguas, Ministerio de Fomento y Obras Públicas, concerning
number and disposition of major irrigators in Ica, December
14, 1957. 4 lvs., copy in possession of citing author and in
the files of the Administración Técnica de las Aguas del Río
Ica.
Castro Pozo, Hildebrando
1947   El yanaconaje en las haciendas piuranas. Recopilación y notas
de Hildebrando A. Castro Pozo. Lima: Compañía de Im-
presiones y Publicidad.
Chabert, F., and L. Dubosc
1908   La viticultura y la vinificación en el departamento de Ica. 2nd
ed., Perú, Ministerio de Fomento, Dirección del Ramo, no.
22, Lima: copy in the Columbus Memorial Library of the
Panamerican Union, Washington, D.C., bound as: Peru,
Misc. Agriculture, Vol. 2, pp. 3–77.
Clark, Margaret
1959   Health in the Mexican-American Culture. Berkeley: The University of California Press.
Cobo, P. Bernabé
1956   Obras de P. Bernabé de Cobo de la Compañía de Jesús. Vol.
I. Estudio preliminar y edición de P. Francisco Mateos de la
misma compañía. Biblioteca de autores españoles desde la
formación del lenguaje hasta nuestros días (Continuación),
Vol. 91, Madrid: Ediciones Atlas.
Collier, John, Jr., and Aníbal Buitrón
1949   The Awakening Valley. Chicago: The University of Chicago
Press.
Conkling, Harold
1939   Explotación de aguas subterraneas en la costa del Perú. Sociedad Nacional Agraria, Junio de 1938, Lima: Imprenta Gil,
S.A.
Crevenna, T. R. (Ed.)
1951   Materiales para el estudio de la clase media en América La-
tina. Publicación de la Oficina de Ciencias Sociales, Wash-
ington: Panamerican Union.
Currier, Richard L.
1966   "The Hot-Cold Syndrome and Symbolic Balance in Mexican
and Spanish-American Folk Medicine." Ethnology 5(3):251–
263.
Davidson, William
1947   "Rural Latin American Culture." Social Forces 25:249–252.
Dawson, L. E.
MS.   Characteristics of Paracas-Nasca Culture. Read in part at the
First Annual Meeting of the Kroeber Anthropological Society.

Berkeley, Calif., May 18, 1957, copy in possession of author.
Dias, Jorge
1948 *Vilarinho da Furna. Uma Aldeia Comunitária.* Porto: Instituto para a Alta Cultura, Centro de Estudos de Etnologia Peninsular.
1953 *Rio de Onor.* Porto: Instituto de Alta Cultura, Centro de Estudos de Etnologia Peninsular.
Donaire Vizarreta, Juan
1941 *Campiña iqueña: aspectos folklóricos.* Lima: Imprenta La Moderna.
Drachmann, A. G.
1932 *Ancient Oil Mills and Presses.* Det Kgl. Danske Videnskabernes Selskab, Archaeologisk-kunsthistoriske Meddelelser, Vol. 1, No. 1, Copenhagen.
Eisenstadt, S. N.
1956 "Ritualized Personal Relations." *Man* 56(96):90–95.
Engel, Frederic
1957 "Early Sites on the Peruvian Coast." *Southwestern Journal of Anthropology* 13:54–68.
Erasmus, Charles J.
MS. *Reciprocal Labor: a Study of its Occurrence and Disappearance among Farming Peoples in Latin America.* Doctoral dissertation submitted at the University of California, Berkeley, 1955, 263 lvs., available on microfilm from the University Library.
1956 "The Occurrence and Disappearance of Reciprocal Farm Labor in Latin America." *Southwestern Journal of Anthropology* 12:449–469.
Escobar M., Gabriel
1964 "Sicaya, una Comunidad Mestiza de la Sierra Central del Perú." In José María Argüedas (Ed.), *Estudios Sobre la Cultura Actual del Perú.* Lima: Universidad Mayor de San Marcos, pp. 150–220.
———, and Gloria Escobar
1954 "Procesos en el contexto social y cultural de las adivinanzas." *Folklore Americano,* Año 2, No. 2, pp. 3–23, Organ del Comité Interamericano del Folklore, Lima.
Fallers, Lloyd A.
1954 "A Note on the 'Trickle Effect.'" *Public Opinion Quarterly* 18:314–321.
Faron, Louis C.
1960 "The Formation of Two Indigenous Communities in Coastal Peru." *American Anthropologist* 62(3):437–453.
Forbes, R. J.
1955 *Studies in Ancient Technology.* Vol. 3, Leiden: E. J. Brill.
Ford, Thomas R.
1955 *Man and Land in Peru.* Gainesville: University of Florida Press.

Foster, George M.
1953a "Relationships between Spanish and Spanish-American Folk Medicine." *Journal of American Folklore* 66:201–217.
1953b "What is Folk Culture?" *American Anthropologist* 55:159–173.
1953c "Confradía and Compadrazgo in Spain and Spanish America." *Southwestern Journal of Anthropology* 9:1–28.
1960 *Culture and Conquest: America's Spanish Heritage.* New York: Wenner-Gren Foundation for Anthropological Research, Inc.
1961 "The Dyadic Contract: A Model for the Social Structure of a Mexican Peasant Village." *American Anthropologist* 63(6):1173–1192.
1963 "The Dyadic Contract II: Patron-Client Relationship." *American Anthropologist* 65(6):1280–1294.
1967 *Tzintzuntzan: Mexican Peasants in a Changing World.* Boston: Little, Brown and Company.
Fried, Jacob
1962 "Social Organization and Personal Security in a Peruvian Hacienda Indian Community: Vicos." *American Anthropologist* 64(4):771–780.
Fuchs, Federico G.
1905 *La región cuprífera de los alrededores de Ica y Nazca.* Perú, Ministerio de Fomento, Boletín del Cuerpo de Ingenieros de Minas del Perú, No. 29, Lima.
Fuentes, Manuel A.
1866 *Lima.* London: Trübner and Co.
Gago, Ezequiel
1919 "Zona de irrigación del Departamento de Ica. Memoria presentada por el Jefe de la Comisión Técnica, Ingeniero Ezequiel Gago." In *Memorias de las Comisiones Técnicas de Aguas. Memoria que el Director de Aguas, Ingo. Alberto Jochamowitz presenta al Ministerio de Fomento,* Vol. 2, 1918–1919, pp. 503–570, Lima. [The published source was unavailable, and all page references in the text are to the MS. copy on file with citing author and in the archives of the Comisión Técnica de las Aguas del Río Ica.]
Garland, A.
n.d. *Peru in 1906 and After.* Lima: La Industria. [Preface is dated 1907.]
Germani, Gino
1965 "The Transition to a Mass Democracy in Argentina." In Dwight B. Heath and Richard N. Adams (Eds.), *Contemporary Cultures and Societies of Latin America.* New York: Random House, pp. 454–472.
Gérol, Harry E.
1961 *Dioses, Templos y Ruinas: Origen, Esplendor y Ocaso del Imperio Inkaico.* Buenos Aires: Librería Hachette S.A.

125

Gillin, John P.
1947a *Moche: a Peruvian Coastal Community.* Smithsonian Institution, Institute of Social Anthropology, Publication No. 3, Washington.
1947b "Modern Latin American Culture." *Social Forces* 25:243–248.
1960   "Some Signposts for Policy." In Council on Foreign Relations (Eds.), *Social Change in Latin America Today.* New York: Harper and Brothers, pp. 14–62.
Goldkind, Victor
1965   "Social Stratification in the Peasant Community: Redfield's Chan Kom Reinterpreted." *American Anthropologist* 67(4): 863–884.
1966   "Class Conflict and Cacique in Chan Kom." *Southwestern Journal of Anthropology* 22(4):325–345.
Goldschmidt, Walter
1950   "Social Class in America — a Critical Review." *American Anthropologist* 52:483–498.
González Herrera, Israel
1944   *Guía general de Ica.* Pisco: Imprenta Merino y Fereyra.
n.d.   *Valle de Ica. Guía general de Ica.* Vol. 2, Pisco: Imprenta Merino y Fereyra.
Hammel, Eugene A.
1959   *Wealth, Authority, and Prestige in the Ica Valley, Peru.* Doctoral dissertation submitted at the University of California, Berkeley, 1959, 275 lvs.
1961   "The Family Cycle in a Coastal Peruvian Slum and Village." *American Anthropologist* 63:989–1005.
1962a *Wealth, Authority and Prestige in the Ica Valley, Peru.* University of New Mexico Publications in Anthropology, No. 10. Albuquerque.
1962b "Social Rank and Evolutionary Position in a Coastal Peruvian Village." *Southwestern Journal of Anthropology* 18:199–215.
1964a "Some Characteristics of Rural Village and Urban Slum Populations on the Coast of Peru." *Southwestern Journal of Anthropology* 20:346–358.
1964b "Culture as an Information System." *Papers of the Kroeber Anthropological Society* 31:89–91.
1964c "Territorial Patterning of Marriage Relationships in a Coastal Peruvian Village." *American Anthropologist* 66:66–74.
MS.   *The Pink Yo-Yo: Occupational Mobility and Economic Growth in Belgrade, ca. 1915–1965. Research Monograph Series,* Institute of International Studies, University of California, Berkeley (in press).
———, A. M. Norsworthy, and John H. Rowe
MS.   *The Epigonal and Chulpaca Pottery Styles of the Ica Valley, Peru.* Copy on file with authors.

Harris, Marvin
1964   *Patterns of Race in the Americas.* New York: Walker and Company.
Hawthorn, Harry B., and Audrey Engle Hawthorn
1948   "Social Stratification in a Latin American City." *Social Forces* 27:19–29.
Hohenthal, W. D.
1959   "Sex, Class, and Status in Racial Relations — Northeast Brazil." *Papers of the Kroeber Anthropological Society* 21:17–24.
Holmberg, Allan R.
1960   "Changing Community Attitudes and Values in Peru: A Case Study in Guided Change." In Council on Foreign Relations (Eds.), *Social Change in Latin America Today.* New York: Harper and Brothers, pp. 63–107.
———, Henry F. Dobyns, and Mario C. Vásquez
1961   "Methods for the Analysis of Cultural Change." *Anthropological Quarterly* 34(2):37–46.
Hudson, Wilson M.
1951   "The Healer of Los Olmos and Other Mexican Lore." Dallas: *Texas Folklore Society Publication* No. 24.
Kelly, Isabel
1956   *Santiago Tuxtla, Vera Cruz: Culture and Health.* Mexico D.F.: Institute of Inter-American Affairs.
1965   *Folk Practices in Northern Mexico.* Austin: The University of Texas Press.
Kenny, Michael
1960   "Patterns of Patronage in Spain." *Anthropological Quarterly* 33:14–23.
Kubler, George
1952   *The Indian Caste of Peru, 1795–1940. A Population Study Based upon Tax Records and Census Reports.* Prepared in cooperation with the United States Department of State as a project of the Interdepartmental Committee on Scientific and Cultural Cooperation, Smithsonian Institution, Institute of Social Anthropology, Publication No. 14, Washington, D.C.
Lanning, Edward P.
MS.   *Chronologies and Cultural Relationships of Early Pottery Styles in Ancient Peru.* Doctoral dissertation submitted at the University of California, Berkeley, 1960, 656 lvs.
1967   *Peru Before the Incas.* Englewood Cliffs: Prentice-Hall.
———, and Eugene A. Hammel
1961   "Early Lithic Industries of Western South America." *American Antiquity* 27:139–154.
Lauria, Anthony, Jr.
1964   " 'Respeto,' 'Relajo' and Inter-Personal Relations in Puerto Rico." *Anthropological Quarterly* 37:53–67.

Lenski, Gerhard
1966   *Power and Privilege: a Theory of Social Stratification.* New York: McGraw-Hill.
Lerner, Daniel
1958   *The Passing of Traditional Society.* Glencoe: The Free Press.
Lewis, Oscar
1959   *Five Families: Mexican Case Studies in the Culture of Poverty.* New York: Basic Books.
1960   *Tepoztlán: Village in Mexico.* New York: Holt, Rinehart and Winston.
1961   *The Children of Sánchez.* New York: Random House.
1965   *La Vida: A Puerto Rican Family in the Culture of Poverty — San Juan and New York.* New York: Random House.
MacLean y Estenós, Roberto
1947   *Negros en el Perú.* Lima.
Madsen, William
1961   *Society and Health in the Lower Rio Grande Valley.* Austin: Hogg Foundation for Mental Health, University of Texas.
1964   *The Mexican-Americans of South Texas.* New York: Holt, Rinehart and Winston.
Mangin, William
1957   "Drinking Among Andean Indians." *Quarterly Journal of Studies on Alcohol* 18:55–66.
1960   "Mental Health and Migration to Cities: A Peruvian Case." In Franklin N. Furness (Ed.), *Culture, Society and Health.* Annals of the New York Academy of Sciences 84(17):911–917.
1964a   "Estratificación Social en el Callejón de Huaylas." In José María Argüedas (Ed.), *Estudios Sobre la Cultura Actual del Perú.* Lima: Universidad Mayor de San Marcos, pp. 16–36.
1964b   "Clubes de Provincianos en Lima." In José María Argüedas (Ed.), *Estudios Sobre la Cultura Actual del Perú.* Lima: Universidad Mayor de San Marcos, pp. 273–297.
1965   "The Role of Regional Associations in the Adaptation of Rural Migrants to Cities in Peru." In Dwight B. Heath and Richard N. Adams (Eds.), *Contemporary Cultures and Societies of Latin America.* New York: Random House, pp. 311–323.
1967   "Squatter Settlements." *Scientific American* 217(4):21–29.
Marie, Victor
1916   *La producción del algodón en el Perú.* Perú, Boletín del Ministerio de Fomento, Año 2, No. 4, Lima.
Marsters, V. F.
1908   "El valle de Ica y su hidrología." In *Dos informes sobre los valles de Ilo, Moquegua, é Ica.* Perú, Ministerio de Fomento, Boletín del Cuerpo de Ingenieros de Minas del Perú, No. 59, pp. 22–43, Lima.
1909   *Informe sobre la costa sur del Perú.* Perú, Ministerio de Fo-

mento, Boletín del Cuerpo de Ingenieros de Minas del Perú, No. 70, Lima.

Martínez, Cervando, and Harry W. Martin
1966 "Folk Diseases Among Urban Mexicans." *The Journal of the American Medical Association* 196(2):161–164.

Martínez Compañón, D. Baltazar Jaime
1936 *Trujillo del Perú a fines del siglo XVIII.* Jesús Domínguez Bordona (Ed.), Madrid.

Martínez, Héctor
1963 "Compadrazgo en una Comunidad Indígena Altiplánica." *América Indígena* 23(2):128–139.
1965 "Los Promotores Sociales en los Programas de Integración." *América Indígena* 25(2):245–256.

Matos, José
1964 "La Propriedad en la Isla de Taquile (Lago Titicaca)." In José María Argüedas (Ed.), *Estudios Sobre la Cultura Actual del Perú.* Lima: Universidad Mayor de San Marcos, pp. 64–142.

Means, Philip A.
1918 "Social Conditions in the Piura-Tumbes Region of Northern Peru." *The Scientific Monthly* 7:385–399.

Menzel, Dorothy
1958 "Problemas en el estudio del horizonte medio en la arqueología peruana." *Revista del Museo Regional de Ica*, Año 9, No. 10, pp. 24–57, Ica.
1959 "The Inca Occupation of the South Coast of Peru." *Southwestern Journal of Anthropology* 15:125–142.
MS. *The Late Ica Pottery of Ancient Peru.* Doctoral dissertation submitted at the University of California, Berkeley, 1954, 248 lvs., available on microfilm from the University Library.

Mintz, Sidney W.
1953 "The Folk-Urban Continuum and the Rural Proletarian Community." *The American Journal of Sociology* 59(2):136–143.
———, and Eric Wolf
1950 "An Analysis of Ritual Co-parenthood (Compadrazgo)." *Southwestern Journal of Anthropology* 6:341–368.

Miró Quesada Sosa, Aurelio
1947 *Costa, sierra y montaña.* Segunda edición aumentada, Lima: Editorial Cultural Antártica, S.A.

Mishkin, Bernardo
1964 "Posesión de la Tierra en la Comunidad de Kauri, Quispicanchis Cuzco." In José María Argüedas (Ed.), *Estudios Sobre la Cultura Actual del Perú.* Lima: Universidad Mayor de San Marcos, pp. 143–149.

Montalvo, Abner
1967 *Sociocultural Change and Differentiation in a Rural Peruvian*

Community: An Analysis in Health Culture. Ithaca: Cornell University.

Montell, Gösta
1929   Dress and Ornaments in Ancient Peru. London: Oxford University Press.

Moore, Sally Falk
1958   Power and Property in Inca Peru. Morningside Heights: Columbia University.

Morúa, Fr. Martín de
1946   Los orígenes de los Incas. Crónica sobre el antiguo Perú escrita en el año de 1590 por el padre mercedario Fr. Martín de Morúa. Los pequeños grandes libros de historia americana, Director F. A. Loayza, Series 1, Vol. 11, Lima: D. Miranda.

Nachtigal, Horst
1964   "El Estado Estamental de los Incas Peruanos." América Indígena 24(2):93–110.

Nadel, S. F.
1951   The Foundations of Social Anthropology. London: Cohen and West.

Nuñez del Prado, Oscar
1955   "Aspects of Andean Native Life." Papers of the Kroeber Anthropological Society 12:1–21. Berkeley.
1964   "El Hombre y la Familia: Su Matrimonio y Organización Politico-Social en Q'ero." In José María Argüedas (Ed.), Estudios Sobre la Cultura Actual del Perú. Lima: Universidad Mayor de San Marcos, pp. 273–297.

Parsons, Elsie Clews
1945   Peguche: A Study of Andean Indians. Chicago: The University of Chicago Press.

Patch, Richard W.
1966   "Fernando Belaunde Terry and Peruvian Politics." In Robert D. Tomasek (Ed.), Latin American Politics. New York: Doubleday.

Patrón, Pablo
1935   Lima antigua. Lima: Imprenta Gil, S.A.

Paulette, Miguel
1953   "Estadística de Ica." Revista del Museo Regional de Ica, Año 5, No. 6, pp. 22–37. With comments by Albert Casa Vilca. Reprinted from El Peruano, Diario Oficial, Año 32, Vol. 2, No. 115, Lima, Lunes, 23 de Noviembre de 1874.

Perú
MS.   Estado geográfico del virreynato del Peru sus yntend.s partid.s doctrin.s pueblos anexos y sus pobladores con distinción de clases y sexos como se manifiesta. 1792 (Census of 1791). Archivo General de Indias, Sevilla, Estado, 75, photographic copies in possession of John H. Rowe.

Perú, Cámara Algodonera
1940–42 *Memoria anual.* Lima, 4 Vols.
1940–55 *Algodón.* Boletín de la Cámara Algodonera del Perú, Nos. 1–184, Lima.
1962 *Memoria anual.* Lima.
Perú, Ministerio de Fomento, Dirección de las Aguas del Río Ica
MS. *Ordenanzas del Río Ica y de la Achirana, 4 de Marzo de 1921.* Original in the archives of the Comisión Técnica, Ica; extract in possession of citing author.
Perú, Ministerio de Fomento, Dirección de Estadística
1919 *Extracto estadístico, 1918.* Lima.
Perú, Ministerio de Gobierno, Dirección de Estadística
1878 *Resúmen del censo general de habitantes del Perú hecho en 1876.* Lima.
Perú, Ministerio de Hacienda y Comercio, Dirección Nacional de Estadística
1935 *Extracto estadístico del Perú, 1931–1932–1933.* Lima.
1942 *Extracto estadístico del Perú.* Lima.
1947 *Anuario estadístico del Perú, 1944–45.* Lima.
1948 *Censo nacional de población de 1940.* Vol. 6: Ica, pp. xv–xxviii, 3–75, Lima.
1958 *Boletín de estadística peruana.* Año 1, No. 1, Lima.
1966a *Censo nacional de población de 1961.* Vol. 1:3, Lima.
1966b *Primer censo agropecuario.* Lima.
Peru Today
1911 "Wine Growing." *Peru Today* 3(4):31, June. Lima: West Coast Publishing Co.
1912 "Agriculture and Irrigation in the Valley of Ica." *Peru Today* 4(9):481–490, December. Lima: West Coast Publishing Co.
Picasso, J. Alfredo
1944 "El cultivo de la vid durante el coloniaje." In González Herrera, 1944:43–62.
Pitt-Rivers, Julian A.
1954 *The People of the Sierra.* New York: Criterion Books.
1957 "The Closed Community and its Friends." *Papers of the Kroeber Anthropological Society*, 16:5–15, Berkeley.
Prado, Javier
1941 *Estado social del Perú durante la dominación española.* Colección de libros y documentos referentes a la historia del Perú, 3rd series, Lima: Librería é Imprenta Gil. (Orig. publ. 1894.)
Preusse-Sperber, O.
1913 *Peru. Eine Skizze seines wirtschaftlichen und staatlichen Lebens.* Angewandte Geographie, Hefte zur Verbreitung geographischer Kentnisse in ihrer Beziehung zum Kultur und Wirtschaftsleben, Hugo Grothe (Ed.), 4th series, pt. 7, O. Preusse-Sperber, New York; Frankfurt a.M.: Verlag Heinrich Keller.

131

Price, Richard
1965 "Trial Marriage in the Andes." *Ethnology* 4(3):310–322.
Prince, Carlos (Ed.)
1890 *Lima antigua.* Lima: Imprenta del Universo de Carlos Prince.
Pursche, Anna
1944 "Scenes of Lima Attributed to Pancho Fierro." *Notes Hispanic* 4:92–132.
Raimondi, Antonio
1945 *Notas de viajes para su obra, El Perú.* Vol. 3, Lima: Imprenta Torres Aguirre.
Romano, Octavio Ignacio
1960 "Donship in a Mexican-American Community in Texas." *American Anthropologist* 62(6):966–976.
1965 "Charismatic Medicine, Folk-Healing, and Folk-Sainthood." *American Anthropologist* 67(5):1151–1173.
Romero, Carlos Alberto
1905 *Negros y caballos.* 3rd ed., Lima: Tipografía Nacional.
Romero, Emilio
1939 *Geografía económica del Perú.* Edición con nuevo apendice, Lima: Imprenta Torres Aguirre.
Rossel Castro, P. Alberto
1954 *Caciques y templos de Ica.* Editado en los talleres de la penitenciaría de Lima.
Rowe, John H.
1946 "Inca Culture at the Time of the Spanish Conquest." In *Handbook of South American Indians,* Julian Steward (Ed.), Smithsonian Institution, Bureau of American Ethnology, Bulletin 143, Vol. 2, pp. 183–330, Washington.
1947 "The Distribution of Indians and Indian Languages in Peru." *Geographical Review* 37:202–215.
1953 "Review of *The Indian Caste of Peru, 1795–1940,* by George Kubler." *Hispanic American Historical Review* 33:92–97.
1957 "The Incas under Spanish Colonial Institutions." *Hispanic American Historical Review* 37:155–199.
1958a "La seriación cronológica de la cerámica de Paracas elaborada por Lawrence E. Dawson." *Revista del Museo Regional de Ica,* Año 9, No. 10, pp. 9–21, Ica.
1958b "Tiempo, estilo y proceso cultural en la arqueología peruana." *Revista Universitaria,* Universidad Nacional del Cuzco, Año 47, No. 115, pp. 79–96, Cuzco.
1963 "Urban Settlements in Ancient Peru." *Ñawpa Pacha* 1:1–27. Reprinted in J. H. Rowe and D. Menzel (Eds.), *Peruvian Archaeology: Selected Readings.* Palo Alto: Peek Publications, 1967.
MS. "A Social Theory of Culture Change." Copy of a paper read to the First Annual Meeting of the Kroeber Anthropological Society, Berkeley, May 18, 1957, 6 lvs., copy in possession of author and citing author.

Rowe, John H., *et al.*
MS. *Notes on a seminar on the role of prestige in intra-societal diffusion, 1957.* Copy in possession of citing author.
Rubel, Arthur J.
1960 "Concepts of Disease in Mexican-American Culture." *American Anthropologist* 62(5):795–814.
1964 "The Epidemiology of a Folk Illness: Susto in Hispanic America." *Ethnology* 3(3):268–283.
Sánchez Elías, Julio Ezequiel
1957 *Cuatro siglos de la historia iqueña.* Lima: Editorial Victory.
Saunders, Lyle
1954 *Cultural Difference and Medical Care.* New York: Russell Sage Foundation.
Sayers, William C.
1956 "Ritual Kinship and Negative Affect." *American Sociological Review* 21(3):348–352.
Schweigger, Erwin
1947 *El litoral peruano.* Lima: Compañía Administradora del Guano.
Simmons, Ozzie G.
1955a "Popular and Modern Medicine in Mestizo Communities of Coastal Peru and Chile." *Journal of American Folklore* 68: 57–71.
1955b "The Criollo Outlook in the Mestizo Culture of Coastal Peru." *American Anthropologist* 57:107–117.
1959 "Drinking Patterns and Interpersonal Performance in a Peruvian Mestizo Community." *Quarterly Journal of Studies on Alcohol* 20(1):103–111.
1960 "Ambivalence and the Learning of Drinking Behavior in a Peruvian Community." *American Anthropologist* 62(6): 1018–1027.
Smelser, Neil J., and Seymour Martin Lipset (Eds.)
1966 *Social Structure and Mobility in Economic Development.* Chicago: Aldine.
Stein, William
1961 *Hualcán: Life in the Highlands of Peru.* Ithaca: Cornell University Press.
Stewart, Watt
1951 *Chinese Bondage in Peru.* Durham: Duke University Press.
Strickon, Arnold
1962 "Class and Kinship in Argentina." *Ethnology* 1(4):500–515.
Strong, William Duncan
1957 "Paracas, Nazca and Tiahuanacoid Cultural Relationships in South Coastal Peru." *Memoirs of the Society for American Archaeology*, No. 13.
Sutton, Carlos W.
1905 *Estudio de un proyecto para irrigar el valle de Ica.* Perú,

Ministerio de Fomento, Boletín del Cuerpo de Ingenieros de Minas del Perú, No. 28, Lima.

1907 *El problema de la irrigación del valle de Ica*. Perú, Ministerio de Fomento, Boletín del Cuerpo de Ingenieros de Minas del Perú, No. 56, Lima.

Tarde, Gabriel de
1895 *Les lois de l'imitation*. 2nd ed., Paris.

Tschudi, J. J. von
1847 *Travels in Peru during the Years 1838–1842*. Thomasina Ross, tr., London: David Brogue.

Tumin, Melvin M.
1952 *Caste in a Peasant Society*. Princeton: Princeton University Press.

Valdizán, Hermilio, and Angel Maldonado
1922 *La medicina popular peruana*. 3 Vols., Lima: Imprenta Torres Aguirre.

Varallanos, José
1962 *El Cholo y el Perú: Introducción al Estudio Sociológico de un Hombre y un Pueblo Mestizos y su Destino Cultural*. Buenos Aires: Imprenta López.

Vásquez, Mario C.
1965 "Changes in the Social Stratification of an Andean Hacienda." In Dwight B. Heath and Richard N. Adams (Eds.), *Contemporary Cultures and Societies of Latin America*. New York: Random House, pp. 405–423.

———, and Allan R. Holmberg
1966 "The Castas: Unilineal Kin Groups in Vicos, Peru." *Ethnology* 5(3):284–303.

Vásquez de Espinosa, Antonio
1948 *Compendia y descripción de las Indias occidentales*. Transcrito por Charles Upson Clark, publicado bajo los auspicios del Comité Interdepartamental de Cooperación Científica y Cultural de los Estado Unidos, Publication 3898, Smithsonian Institution, Miscellaneous Collections, Vol. 108, Washington.

Veblen, Thorstein
1953 *The Theory of the Leisure Class*. New York: Mentor Books. (Orig. publ. 1899.)

Wagley, Charles (Ed.)
1963 *Race and Class in Rural Brazil*. Holland: UNESCO.

Wagley, Charles
1965 "On the Concept of Social Race in the Americas." In Dwight B. Heath and Richard N. Adams (Eds.), *Contemporary Cultures and Societies of Latin America*. New York: Random House, pp. 531–545.

———, and Marvin Harris
1955 "A Typology of Latin American Subcultures." *American Anthropologist* 57:428–451.

Weber, Max
1958   "Class, Status, Party." In Hans H. Gerth and C. Wright
       Mills (Eds.), *From Max Weber: Essays in Sociology*. New
       York: Oxford University Press.
Weberbauer, August
1945   *El mundo vegetal de los Andes peruanos: estudio fitogeográ-*
       fico. Nueva edición, revisada y ampliada de Die Pflanzenwelt
       der peruanischen Anden, Leipzig: Wilhelm Engelmann,
       1911. Lima: Ministerio de Agricultura, Dirección de Agri-
       cultura, Estación Experimental Agrícola de la Molina.
Wellin, Edward
MS.   *Processes of Directed Culture Change: Studies of Health*
       Action in Peru. Doctoral dissertation submitted to Harvard
       University, 1955, available on microfilm from University Mi-
       crofilms, Ann Arbor, extracts and relevant material published
       in the following two entries.
1953   "Pregnancy, Childbirth, and Midwifery in the Valley of Ica,
       Peru." *Health Information Digest for Hot Countries* 3(1):
       1–51. London: Central Council for Health Education ("An
       abbreviated version of a memorandum by Edward Wellin
       . . . June, 1953.").
1955   "Water Boiling in a Peruvian Town." In Benjamin D. Paul
       (Ed.), *Health, Culture and Community*. New York: The
       Russell Sage Foundation, pp. 71–106.
Whiteford, Andrew Hunter
1960   *Two Cities of Latin America.* Beloit College: The Logan
       Museum of Anthropology, Bulletin Number Nine.
Whitten, Norman E., Jr.
1965   *Class, Kinship, and Power in an Ecuadorian Town: The Ne-*
       groes of San Lorenzo. Stanford: Stanford University Press.
Willey, Gordon R.
1953   *Prehistoric Settlement Patterns in the Virú Valley, Perú.*
       Smithsonian Institution, Bureau of American Ethnology,
       Bulletin 155, Washington.
1958   "Estimated Correlations and Dating of South and Central
       American Culture Sequences." *American Antiquity* 23:353–
       378.
Wolf, Eric R.
1955   "Types of Latin American Peasantry: a Preliminary Discus-
       sion." *American Anthropologist* 57:452–471.
1956   "Aspects of Group Relations in a Complex Society: Mexico."
       American Anthropologist 58:1065–1078.
Wright, Marie Robinson
1908   *The Old and the New Peru.* Philadelphia: Geo. Barrie & Sons.
Zeuner, Frederick E.
1963   *A History of Domesticated Animals.* London: Hutchinson of
       London.

135

Glossary

acequia — irrigation ditch.

achira — a sweet edible root, *Canna edulis*.

aguardiente — literally, burning water or fire-water, a generic term for distilled alcoholic beverages of high proof, but applied in Ica more to distillates of cane (*cañazo*) than to *pisco*.

agua de mandamiento — special, emergency irrigation water sent past upper feeder ditch inlets to lower ones, in temporary suspension of the rule of *cabecera*.

ahijado — godchild, godson (fem., *ahijada*).

alambique — a still for making *aguardiente*, having a coiled exhaust tube (see *serpentín*).

alcalde — in Ica the appointed chief administrative officer of a municipality.

aparcería — sharecropping (see *yanaconaje*).

barriada — a *barrio* or section of a city inhabited by the lower classes, a slum, sometimes a squatters' quarter.

bestia — beast.

bien criollo — really creole, or really modern in outlook and style.

blanco — white, also European.

136

botija — pottery wine jar, amphora.

brujo — male witch or magical curer (fem., *bruja*).

cabecera — a legal term in irrigation law in Ica, denoting priority in access to water, according to relative closeness to the *cabeza* or head of a ditch.

cachina — young, newly fermented wine.

cacique — a chief; the term was applied to local nobles in the colonial period.

caciquismo — a style of governance characterized by graft and the exercise of personal influence.

cañazo — *aguardiente* made from sugar cane, a cheap and fiery white rum.

cancate — a coarse garden pea, *Pisum sativum* var.

cancha — kernels of maize roasted in hot sand.

cantina — a bar or restaurant where drinks are served.

Capitán — the military title of Captain, but also the name of a cocktail made with *pisco* and sweet vermouth, like a Manhattan.

caudillo — a political boss or strong man.

cebiche — a dish made of raw fish by soaking fillets of fish several hours in lemon juice with raw onions and hot peppers.

chalet — in Ica, a style of house made of whitewashed adobe or concrete, of one story, and having a small enclosed garden at the front, surrounded by a fence made of concrete and iron grille.

chicha — a beer made of maize, although sometimes also a sweet non-alcoholic beverage made by boiling purple maize with fruits (*chicha morada*).

chifa — a restaurant serving Chinese dishes.

cholo — in Ica, a member of the lower class, a peasant, but not a highlander.

colectivo — a jitney, a taxi with a fixed route.

comadre — co-mother, a term applied mutually between a mother and the godmother of her child, by a godfather to the mother, or by a father to the godmother.

compadrazgo — co-parenthood, the social relationship or institution centering around baptismal and similar types of sponsorship.

compadre — co-father, a term applied mutually between a father and the godfather of his child, by a godmother to the father, or by a mother to the godfather.

compañía — partnership, applied in Ica to a type of sharecropping in which the participants share fairly equally.

concejal — councilman, alderman.

corral — an enclosed pen or room for fowl or other livestock.

corregidor — a Spanish provincial official, appointed to oversee an administrative jurisdiction, either of Spaniards and others or of Indians.

criollismo — a term applied to the cultural style of modern coastal Peru, contrasting with the Indian heritage and also with the North American and European traditions, a "Latin" cultural blend.

criollo — creole, having the qualities of *criollismo*.

curandero — a male curer, usually one who works with herbal remedies rather than by magic (see *brujo*) (fem., *curandera*).

empleado — an employee receiving a monthly salary rather than an hourly wage, usually a person in a white-collar occupation.

encomendero — in the colonial period a Spaniard holding a grant of authority over an area of land and its inhabitants, imposing on him the obligation to collect royal tribute and allowing certain exploitative privileges.

escabeche — a spicy dish made of pickled fish or poultry.

falca — a pot still for making *aguardiente*, having a straight exhaust tube (see *alambique, serpentín*).

fútbol — the game of soccer.

garúa — a very heavy fog or drizzling mist, commonest in Ica in June and July (the winter).

gobernador — the appointed administrative official of a local district.

guinda — cherry.

hacendado — owner of a large agricultural property or hacienda.

huayno — a highland Indian dance form and associated dance music.

indígena — native, aboriginal.

indio — Indian.

jíquima — tuber bean (*Pachyrhizus erosus*).

llamador — in Ica a magical curer specializing in calling the lost souls of children through a series of magical acts (see *susto*).

lúcuma — a fruit (*Lucuma obovata*).

machismo — the quality of maleness in personality, involving personal dominance, show, courage, and sexual exploit.

madrina — the term used by a godchild (or married person) to refer to the godmother (or female marriage sponsor); the sponsored person is *ahijado* or *ahijada* to the *madrina*, and the *madrina* is *comadre* to the parents of the sponsored person.

malcriado — a person of rude manners, poorly brought up.

mal ojo — the evil eye.

marinera — a dance form popular in the republican and early modern period, still popular in the highlands, now reintroduced in Lima in a folkloristic revival.

mataperro — literally, dog-killer, a term of disapprobation applied to rich ne'er-do-wells of the republican period who were involved in the emerging *criollo* culture.

mayorala — a woman holding the equivalent of a *mayordomo*'s position as head of a *mayordomía*, or lay religious organization.

mayordomía — a Catholic lay association with duties in the financing and management of fiestas.

mayordomo — a man holding the post of head of a *mayordomía*.

mestizo — a person of mixed blood, originally one of Spanish and Indian ancestry but now applied to mixtures involving Negroes, Chinese, etc.; also a term for the mixture of European and indigenous cultures or a person participating in this mixed cultural tradition.

misa de gallo — Christmas midnight mass.

mita — in Inca and colonial times, a system of corvée labor; in modern Ica, a system of allocation of time for irrigation when water is scarce, in suspension of the usual rule of *cabecera*.

mora — blackberry.

mujer — woman, wife.

norteamericano — North American, usually applied only to citizens of the United States and not to Canadians.

pacay — alternate, *pacae*, a tree with a large, edible, bean-like fruit (*Inga feuillei*).

padrino — the term used by a godchild (or married person) to refer to the godfather (or male marriage sponsor); the sponsored person is *ahijado* or *ahijada* to the *padrino*, and the *padrino* is *compadre* to the parents of the sponsored person.

partidario — a sharecropper or tenant farmer, in partnership with an *hacendado*.

patrón — patron or boss, applied to *hacendados* and also to urban employers.

pepino — melon pear (*Solanum muricatum*).

pisco — a clear brandy, seldom colored, of about 80 proof, made from wine and named for the port from which it was originally shipped: Pisco brandy.

pistaco — in local mythology, a North American engaged in kidnapping Indians to sell their bodies for making grease.

poza — a small irrigation or settlement basin, used to hold flood waters so that crops can be planted subsequently in the floor of the basin.

quincha — a house-construction technique employing cane and mud in wattle-and-daub.

quinoa — goosefoot (*Chenopodium quinoa*).

reducción — in colonial Peru a nucleated settlement established to effect better control over the Indian population; an Indian reservation.

regidor — a local councilman or *concejal*.

reja — a wooden or wrought-iron window grille.

rezador — a magical curer who prays over a sick person to draw out the illness, often into himself, as illustrated by the fact that he sometimes suffers violent nausea following a cure; the word is from *rezar*, to pray.

seco — a dish of boiled rice or bean paste, sometimes topped with meat, fish, or fried egg; from the word meaning "dry," in contrast to the soup that accompanies it.

serpentín — a still for making *aguardiente*, having a coiled exhaust tube (see *alambique, falca*).

serrano — a highland Indian.

sociedad mercantil — a commercial corporation, company.

susto — a disease, usually of children, involving temporary loss of the soul and symptoms of listlessness, fever, loss of appetite and diarrhea. *Susto* is caused by sudden fright at a loud noise or movement, and is cured by a *llamador* who goes to a lonely place to call the sick person's soul by name (hence *llamador*, from *llamar*, to call), entices the soul back to the person's house by dragging an article of the person's clothing behind him, and finally throws the clothing into the house and shuts the door on it, thereby trapping the soul in the same house with the sick person.

tamal — in Ica, a corn husk stuffed with corn meal (sometimes sweetened) and boiled.

teniente-gobernador — an administrative official under a *gobernador*.

torna — a system of labor exchange in which peasants help one another with heavy farm tasks.

transición — the first year of elementary school.

tu — the familiar pronoun of address (thou).

Usted — the formal pronoun of address (you).

vals criollo — a modern dance step, a waltz, and the associated music.

venta — in colonial times, an inn or place of roadside business.

vino generoso — a mature wine fortified with *pisco* to prevent spoilage.

yanaconaje — the institution of sharecropping or tenant farming, the state of being a *yanacona* or tenant farmer.

yanacona — in Inca times, a member of the hereditary caste of craftsmen; in later times, a tenant farmer or sharecropper.

yuca — sweet manioc (*Manihot utilissima*).

Index

godparenthood, 69–70, 76, 79, 84, 90–91, 94, 96, 101
Gutiérrez, Emilio (pseudonym), 71–77, 80, 84, 98

housing, 12–13, 66, 72, 77, 80, 86–87, 91–92, 95, 98–99
Huamaní, Hacienda, 6, 12, 16, 26, 48

Ica River, 8n
irrigation, 8, 13, 21n, 26–30, 116 (see also well water)
Italians, 35, 38, 40, 57, 58–59, 60, 70, 77–80

labor: control of, 111; cooperative, 25, 111; migrant, 17, 22; skilled, 31, 41–42, 59–60, 63, 113; slave, 11, 16, 17, 111
land, distribution of, 16, 20–22
liquor, distillation of, 32–38 passim

marriage: common-law, 84–86; patterns of, 49–50
mayordomía, 100, 101
medical care, 69, 75, 79, 83, 90, 94–95, 97, 100–101
mobility, social, 1, 52, 119–120; avenues of, 114; group, 4, 112; individual, 4, 114, 116
Mosayguate, Andrés (pseudonym), 98–103

Negroes, 11, 16, 54, 55, 57–58, 69, 71, 103–104n

Ocucaje, Hacienda, 6

Pan-American Highway, 12, 47, 49
partidario (see sharecropping)
parties, political, 3, 108
Pisco River, 8, 29
Pizarro, 10
population, 10, 11–12n
pottery, 10, 33–34, 43–44
power: definition of, 51–52; distribution of, 3, 55–56; political, 106,

power, political (Cont.) 108–110, 118–119; structure of, 53
prestige, 64–65, 114–118; distribution of, 3, 118; symbols of, 53
prostitution, 83

rainfall, 6–8, 27
religious practices, 68–69, 75, 78–79, 83, 89–90, 97, 100
renting of land, 24
Revolution against Spain, 11
Romero, Pedro (pseudonym), 84–91, 94, 96

sex, 79
sharecropping, 16, 17, 22–25, 58, 111
slaves (see labor, slave)
soccer, 81, 94, 101
social activities, 68, 74–75, 78, 82–84, 89, 96, 101–102
social structure, 3, 57, 118–119
Soldán, Enrique (pseudonym), 65–71
Soria, Marcos and Pablo (pseudonyms), 91–95, 96
status, 63n
status groups, 3

Tipacti, Juan (pseudonym), 95–98
torna (see labor, cooperative)
transportation, 11, 13, 43–49, 60, 67, 72–74, 77–78, 81, 87, 99

urbanization, 11–12n, 31

Vasco, Jorge (pseudonym), 80–84, 97
viticulture, 15–16, 18 (see also liquor, distillation of; wine-making)

wealth, distribution of, 3, 52, 55–56, 110–114, 118–119
well water, 8, 28, 29–30, 72, 107 (see also irrigation)
wine-making, 32–33, 34–35, 37–38

yanaconas (see sharecropping)